talking about
evangelism
a congregational resource

holy conversations

A study tool for theological reflection around debates in the church that considers scripture, tradition, reason, and experience.

talking about
evangelism
a congregational resource

D. Mark Davis

THE
PILGRIM
PRESS
Cleveland

To Chris

The Pilgrim Press
700 Prospect Avenue
Cleveland, Ohio 44115-1100
thepilgrimpress.com

♻ Printed in the United States of America on acid-free paper that contains 30% post-consumer fiber.

12 11 10 09 08 07   5 4 3 2 1

Library of Congress Cataloging-in-Publication Data
Davis, D. Mark, 1960-
    Talking about evangelism : a congregational resource / D. Mark Davis.
      p. cm.
    Includes bibliographical references and index.
    ISBN 978-0-8298-1739-3 (alk. paper)
    1. Evangelistic work. 2. Witness bearing (Christianity) I. Title.
    BV3790.D4144 2007
    269'.2 – dc22
                                                        2006036285

Contents

Preface

"Talking about evangelism" may be difficult for many persons of faith, but it is very dear to the heart of this writer. Part of my passion for talking about evangelism comes from my own faith development. I was raised in an evangelistic church tradition, where the commitment to evangelism was paramount. Sermons regularly extolled the Great Commission; traveling evangelists came twice a year to hold revivals; young people were expected to get saved once they had attained the age of accountability; and Christian education included learning such evangelism tools as "the Four Spiritual Laws" and "the Roman Road to Salvation." Moreover, in high school I was part of an ecumenical youth group that would occasionally travel to the mall and go out two by two looking for people with whom to strike up conversations in order to win souls for the kingdom of heaven. After high school I attended a Bible college, where my first semester included a class called "Evangelism 101."

For some readers, this brief narrative might sound like a description of a church that they love dearly. To others, it may sound like a description of their worst nightmare of a church, filled with coded language and presumption. I offer this narrative sympathetically, but critically. I learned many things from the church experience of my youth, things that continue to be meaningful and positive for my ongoing journey of faith.

Nonetheless, throughout this entire phase of my early faith journey, I was never quite at home or comfortable with the language and practice of evangelism that I was taught. I remember vividly wishing that I had never ventured into evangelism at all in response to a very gracious woman, whom I met on an evangelism excursion at a mall. I was thoroughly humbled when she pulled her sleeve back to show me the tattoo that "Christians" had given her at a concentration camp in Germany when she was a child. We ended up having a wonderful conversation, but only because of her kindness.

My discomfort was part of what led me to leave the tradition of my childhood and to join the Presbyterian Church (USA). It was not an easy transition and I continue to appreciate and enjoy certain commitments that were instilled in me during my young life — like my interest in evangelism. However, I know that for me to embrace evangelism means that I need to reassess it from head to toe, examining not only the practice and language of evangelism, but the theology behind it. Thus, this book is a part of my own journey and need to "redeem evangelism" from models and assumptions that are unworthy of a loving, active God and the people whom God calls as disciples through Jesus Christ.

In addition to addressing my own needs, this book is an offering for others who struggle with the call to evangelism. It is not exactly a "how to" book, because a book dedicated to technique would simply put a happier face on evangelism and would miss the opportunity to reevaluate the principles that lie behind the practice of evangelism. It is also not exactly a theological treatise on evangelism, because such texts often come to grand conclusions that still leave the reader with awkward, ongoing questions of practice. Instead, this book is an invitation for people of faith to join together in a "holy conversation" with the intention of redeeming the language and practice of evangelism, based on sound and faithful theological reflection.

Among other great contributions that John Wesley has given to the Christian Church are his "quadrilateral" touchstones for theological reflection: scripture, reason, experience, and tradition. These touchstones are effective tools for community-building as well as for study, so I have included them in various ways for each Discussion Guide. By including "experience" among the more traditional three-legged stool of scripture, reason, and tradition, Wesley has given us a way of inviting candor about our own experiences as a key ingredient for serious reflection.

The wonderful thing about conversations is that one never presumes to have a final word. Every conversation can be picked up again and extended. It is my hope that this book offers you a conversation that you can visit throughout your life. I know I will.

Acknowledgments

It is only fitting to acknowledge that a book on conversing about evangelism is itself the result of many such conversations. Indeed, I am indebted to many people for their insights, questions, passions, and doubts about our call to share the joy and justice of the gospel. In particular, I have had the privilege of serving as the pastor of a wonderful, creative, and inclusive congregation for the last ten years. Heartland Presbyterian Church is a community where honesty and forthrightness are expressions of abiding trust in God's grace.

Also, for the last three years I have found a stimulating fellowship among other pastors as a part of the West Coast Pastor-Theologian Group through the Center of Theological Inquiry in Princeton. This group has been a thoughtful community, in the best sense of both words. My thanks to both my church and my colleagues for frank discussions about salvation and loving encouragement in my endeavors.

The Pilgrim Press has a real gem in the person of Ulrike Guthrie. Uli's prompt, insightful responses as an editor, couched in unfailing kindness, have made the writing process enjoyable and rewarding.

Finally, but most importantly, my wife, Chris, and our four children, Mickey, Luke, Nicholas, and Abby, have made many accommodations to enable this project. Not the least of their indulgences is to put up with a spouse and dad who grinds coffee and stirs around trying to do godly things at ungodly hours. More than anything the people in my family have taught me the joy and justice of God's grace.

Introduction

The Quandary of Evangelism

"Evangelism" seems to be such an awkward term among many people of faith today. Simply defined, evangelism is the activity of sharing the joy and justice of the gospel. As such, it would seem to be an activity that people of faith would do naturally and with a good will. In fact, the scriptures are quite clear that evangelism is an activity at the heart of the Christian church. After his resurrection, Jesus issued what is often called the "Great Commission," charging his followers to go and "make disciples" of many nations. In the scriptures at least, an essential part of one's life as a follower of Jesus Christ is to engage in evangelism.

The Great Commission

"Go therefore and make disciples of all nations, baptizing them in the name of the Father and of the Son and of the Holy Spirit, and teaching them to obey everything that I have commanded you."
— Matthew 28:19–20

However, in many real-life experiences, evangelism appears to be an act of coercion, a forced attempt to change the way another person thinks and lives, that is unnaturally awkward for both parties involved. Ironically, the attempt to follow the Great Commission seems to violate Jesus' "Great Commandment" to love

God and to love one's neighbor as oneself. Hence, even the word "evangelism" has become what many people of faith jokingly call "the E word" — a word that carries such negative connotations that one loathes to say it.

The Great Commandment

"Teacher, which commandment in the law is the greatest?" Jesus said, "You shall love the Lord your God with all your heart, and with all your soul, and with all your mind.... And a second is like it: You shall love your neighbor as yourself."

— Matthew 22:36 – 40

Clearly there is a quandary regarding evangelism: Something that should be a joyous, natural activity for those who follow Christ appears to be a forced, coercive activity unfitting for those who follow Christ. But to dispense with the idea of evangelism seems to be contrary to the nature of being a disciple — at least as discipleship is described in the life of the early church. What results is a spectrum of Christianity with a very confused stance toward evangelism, which might be broadly delineated in the following ways:

- Some persons of faith zealously spread the gospel, but seem to trample on other people's sensitivities and to act un-Christian in the process.

- Some persons of faith pointedly reject the language and activity of evangelism altogether, no matter how biblical or germane to Christianity it seems to be.

- Some persons of faith simply take a very passive approach, neither actively rejecting nor actively practicing evangelism.

Each of these responses to evangelism is understandable, but none of them seems completely satisfying or faithful to the whole calling of Christian discipleship.

The Purpose of This Book

This book offers a way for people of faith to work together to overcome the quandary of evangelism. By sharing experiences, faithfully reflecting, studying the scriptures, and being guided by the wisdom of our traditions, this book will offer small discussion groups an alternative to coercively practicing, outright rejecting, or passively ignoring evangelism. The hope is that each participant will find a voice for sharing the joy and justice of the gospel, practicing faithful and loving ways to follow both the Great Commission *and* the Great Commandment. In short, participants are invited to join together in redeeming evangelism from the unworthy principles and practices that have become associated with it.

The Topics for Discussion

This book is divided into six sessions, structured to guide participants in their journey together. Each session begins with a brief story to introduce the topic of the session.

The first session diagnoses the quandary of evangelism, starting with sharing stories of our own encounters with evangelism. As a result, this session focuses specifically on the *negative* experiences that participants have had with evangelism in order to explore the coercive nature of most models of evangelism.

The second session takes a close look at the Great Commission from Matthew's Gospel and deconstructs the popular reading of it. By being attentive to Luke's various expressions of the Great Commission, we see that Matthew's version of that call is primarily about Christ's abiding presence with the early church.

The third session invites participants to begin imagining a positive conception of evangelism that is not coercive in principle because it is built on the belief that Christ is already redemptively present in the world. That starting point allows for a model of evangelism that carries the kind of respect and candor that is found in honest conversations. The third session, then, explores the role of "genuine listening" as a critical, but often neglected, part of evangelism.

The fourth session focuses on the interdependence of listening and speaking, particularly in finding appropriate and meaningful ways to speak of Jesus Christ, the "evangel" of evangelism.

The fifth session explores different ways of telling our "three-storied experience" as a witness to the grace of God in the world.

The sixth session returns to the quandary of evangelism. The most important question for this final session is whether or not the participants have discovered together a more promising way of practicing evangelism that avoids the kinds of coercion that characterizes most models of evangelism.

The Process for Discussion

For each session there is a corresponding Discussion Guide at the end of the book. These guides are written with the assumption that participants in the study will take turns leading the discussions. When there is some "carry-over" from one week's discussion to the next, it is clearly marked.

It is my hope that each participant will conclude this holy conversation with a renewed commitment to enjoying and sharing the grace of God made known in Jesus Christ and experienced in our life stories. To get there, we must first face the quandary of evangelism together. We will meet current models of coercive evangelism with unsparing criticism as unworthy and presumptuous misrepresentations of God. At the same time, we will turn neither to the outright rejection of evangelism nor to passively ignoring evangelism as a faithful alternative. My hope is that each participant will find loving and meaningful ways to share the joy and justice of the gospel in a world that, however broken, continues to be embraced and called by a gracious and loving God.

talking about
evangelism
a congregational resource

Diagnosing the Quandary of Evangelism

Introduction: *Evangelizing Sam*

He was my favorite high school teacher, the director of our school plays, and we got along marvelously. With his boisterous laugh, his irreverent humor, and his genuine concern about his students, Sam was one of the few teachers that I wanted to visit when I came home from college for my first winter break. He was in his office, feet on his desk, reading the paper until he saw me and swept me up in a bear hug, inviting me to "sit a spell and tell me all about college." Exactly the words I had been hoping to hear.

What Sam was about to find out was that I had taken Evangelism 101 in college and I had come, not only to visit, but also "to seek and to save the lost." I cared about Sam and, from the theological perspective that I embraced at that time, I genuinely worried about the present condition and eternal destiny of his soul. So as soon as the opportunity arose, I followed the directions that I had been taught. I told Sam that I had been thinking of him and wanted to introduce him to Jesus Christ.

To his credit, Sam was very polite during this strange turn of our conversation, a politeness that I took to mean that I was getting somewhere with him. But as polite as he was, he was not quite willing to play along as the textbooks had described. My words to him must not have been convincing, because my entreaties for him to give me a chance to pray "the sinner's prayer" with him were not successful. So after finally having run out of options, I simply said, "Don't worry, I'm praying for you, Sam."

Then Sam exploded. In a sanitized version, his words were something like, "Take your prayers and your holier-than-thou attitude and get the hell out of my office! And don't bother coming back until you leave that crap at home!" And that was it. I drove home shaken, knowing that I had followed precisely the evangelism method that I had been taught. In fact, some of the textbooks prepared us for rejection, explaining that the sinful mind is often hostile to the good news of the gospel. But despite what the textbooks said, I felt deep inside that I had done something terribly wrong.

Sharing Experiences: Exploring Our Own "Evangelism Encounters"

I did not intend my "evangelism encounter" with Sam to be confrontational, but it certainly ended up that way. There were two of us in that room, two lives, two ways of seeing things, and one agenda — mine — that required the other person to change in order to be "saved." Face-to-face encounters offer the greatest possibilities both for sharing love and life and for violating love and life. That is why "personal evangelism" has been both exceedingly effective *and* has done irreparable damage to the good news of the gospel.

Most of us have had some kind of "evangelism encounter" in our life. In preparation for the conversation of the first session, take some time to think about an evangelism encounter that you have had in order to explore the *personal* dynamics involved. Perhaps you were in my shoes, as the "evangelist" of the encounter. If so, try to name the *intentions* that you carried with you into that conversation, specifically exploring what motivated you to introduce or pursue this conversation. Perhaps you were in Sam's shoes, as the "evangelized" person in the encounter. If so, try to name the *feelings* that you had at the time, as well as the feelings that you now have about the encounter in retrospect. Be ready to share with your discussion group the story of your evangelism encounter, as well as your observations regarding the intentions and feelings involved.

Hashing It Out: The Principle behind the Practice

The Episcopal bishop John Shelby Spong has expressed a view of evangelism that strikes a chord with many folks who have been on the receiving end of an awkward or offensive evangelism encounter. With typical candor, Bishop Spong says:

> *Evangelistic efforts and missionary enterprises are . . . compromised by a lack of integrity and filled, despite the veneer of virtuous religious jargon, with manifestations of hostility. I think the Christian Church should abandon these tactics forthwith as unworthy of the Christ figure. I want no part of a "decade of evangelism," or those perennial misguided Christian attempts to convert the Jews. That activity grows out of a sense that one tradition possesses the sole route to God. It reflects a tribal mentality that cannot be a part of our post-theistic world.*[1]

Bishop Spong's call to abandon evangelism is one response to the offensive nature of many evangelistic efforts. Another response is to look for productive and loving ways to embrace evangelism. But, in my mind, there is enough honest truth in Bishop Spong's criticisms of evangelism that it can only be embraced after some hard work of rethinking the activity and language of evangelism from top to bottom, taking Bishop Spong's criticisms very seriously. Toward that end, we will explore the distinction between a model of evangelism that is confrontational *in principle*, versus a model of evangelism that is built on a better understanding of grace.

Of course, it is always possible that a person lacking wisdom or sensitivity might be overzealous in sharing the good news of the gospel, regardless of the model he or she is following. Application is dependent on one's personality and disposition, but even a pleasant personality cannot redeem a model of evangelism that is built on the wrong principles. What we are searching for is a model of evangelism that is adequately grounded in the capacious love and grace of God. By diagnosing the quandary of evangelism, we want to explore how something entitled "good news" has acquired such a negative reputation, and do something to formulate a way of sharing the good news of the gospel that is indeed worthy of the Christ figure.

For example, in my encounter with Sam, I was working from quite a few questionable presumptions. With my intention of "introducing Sam to Jesus Christ," I was assuming that there was no relationship between Sam and Jesus Christ already. Having experienced his irreverent humor, particularly as it was frequently directed at organized religion, I assumed that Sam was hostile to the gospel (a frequent and disastrous confusion between the gospel and the church!). Most disturbingly, I gave no attention to the possibility that God had visited Sam's life in numerous ways long before I ever showed up ready for evangelism.

It may be that much of the offense in my encounter with Sam was simply due to the immaturity of my youth. The more important question is whether my model of evangelism was offensive *in principle*, and not just in application. What kind of theology — that is, what kind of working understanding of God before humanity and humanity before God — was behind my efforts to evangelize? That theological question makes all the difference in the world in whether a model of evangelism is inherently offensive or just a good model poorly executed.

Faithful Reflections: Listening to Our Traditions

Our theological task is to investigate the understanding of God that is at play in our practice of evangelism. In preparation for this task, I invite you to think about the differing ways that your faith tradition expresses an understanding of God by following these three steps:

First, identify your favorite hymn or song of the church. What does your song say about God's stance toward humanity and humanity's standing before God?

Here is one example. In the church that I serve, we sing the first verse of a song called "When We Are Living" (or "Pues Si Vivimos")[2] at every baptism and at every funeral. The text is,

> When we are living, it is in Christ Jesus,
> and when we're dying, it is in the Lord.
> Both in our living and in our dying,
> we belong to God. We belong to God.

When we sing these words at the baptism of a child, they express God's way of calling and claiming us long before we are culpable for our actions or capable of exercising faith. Likewise, when we sing it at a funeral, it speaks of a God who is faithful to us, even beyond our finite life. When we put together the text of the song and the context in which we sing it, it speaks powerfully about God's care for us as both the first and last word of our living.

Second, what do the prayers in your tradition's liturgy, or your own favorite prayers, suggest about God's way of being present in our world?

Even a popular children's table blessing can say something profound and meaningful. To begin a prayer with the twin lines "God is great, God is good" is to begin with two of the most significant claims about God from the Hebrew tradition. "God is great," the powerful creator and sustainer of the world whose ways are higher than our ways. And yet we approach God with boldness because "God is good," merciful and slow to anger, inclined toward us with grace and love. Almost every good prayer, especially the memorable ones, says something significant about God in relation to humanity.

Finally, consider how these theological expressions compare or contrast with the theology behind the practice of evangelism. To help with this step, we will examine a very popular tool of evangelism below.

A Study of Scripture: The Roman Road

One of the most popular methods used for training evangelists throughout the late twentieth century was a collection of scriptures from Paul's letter to the church in Rome called "The Roman Road to Salvation." The idea is that these scripture verses show the significant steps toward salvation, which the evangelist can use to help someone see the need and hear the invitation to accept Jesus Christ as Lord and Savior. By taking a close look at the selection, order, and content of these verses, we will be able to examine the understanding of humanity before God and God before humanity that lies behind many models of evangelism. Here is the "Roman Road" in its most popular form.

The Roman Road to Salvation

Romans 3:23 "For all have sinned and fall short of the glory of God."

Romans 6:23 "For the wages of sin is death, but the gift of God is eternal life through Jesus Christ our Lord."

Romans 5:8 "God demonstrated God's own love for us, in that while we were yet sinners Christ died for us."

Romans 10:9 "If you confess with your mouth the Lord Jesus Christ, and believe in your heart that God has raised him from the dead, you shall be saved."

In order to prepare for your group analysis of the "Roman Road," review the questions below. I am offering some of my own first reactions to the questions for your consideration as well.

* *Out of all of the contents of Paul's letter to Rome, why are these texts specifically selected for evangelism?*

There are quite a few strengths to this selection of texts. They are fairly memorable; they are sequential, so they seem to be following the flow of Paul's letter to the church in Rome; they move efficiently from one idea to another in a journey-like fashion; and they communicate the kind of certainty to which many people are attracted, especially when they feel lost or confused. As a result, these texts provide a simple formula for leading people to the point of accepting Jesus Christ as one's Lord and Savior.

* *Is it the typical New Testament model of evangelism to begin with human sinfulness and its status of condemnation? What other texts or models come to mind?*

One of the most popular "conversion" stories in the Bible is the story of the one who writes this letter to the Romans. In Acts 9 (repeated in Acts 22 and 26), Saul of Tarsus experiences the dramatic change from being an enemy and persecutor of the Christian church to becoming Paul, one of the church's chief apostles. At least from the thumbnail telling of that story it does appear that the "template" of a conversion road is that one begins by being lost in sin before one's life is dramatically changed in a moment of salvation.

However, there is more to Saul's dramatic conversion on the road to Damascus than meets the eye. It is true, according to Paul's accounts of his conversion in Acts 22 and 26, that he had been an enemy of the church. But he was not someone who felt the weight of sin and guilt. In his recorded testimony, Paul says, "Brothers, up to this day I have lived my life with a clear conscience before God." Since that is the case, it is hard to say that Paul's conversion story begins with the words "All have sinned and fall short of the glory of God." Even the dramatic Saul-turned-to-Paul's conversion story invites us to rethink sinfulness and condemnation as the first step on the journey of salvation.

♦ *What kind of claim is one making about God before humanity and humanity before God if the first step of the "Roman Road" begins by declaring the fallen and accursed state of humanity? What other claims about God and humanity come to your mind as a better "first step" to share with others?*

The twentieth-century theologian Paul Tillich describes "sinfulness" as "estrangement," arguing that humanity experiences itself as being estranged from God and, therefore, estranged from one another and even from ourselves.[3] "Estrangement" is a key term because it assumes a prior relationship that has been broken. Therefore, while "sinfulness-as-estrangement" is a powerful way of describing the human situation, it cannot be the "first step" on the human journey because "estrangement" itself assumes a prior relationship. It is that prior relationship that is and always should be identified as the first step for any person's life journey. One way of expressing that prior relationship is to say to each and all, "You are a beloved child of God" as the first step of the human journey.

Now you have read some of my initial responses to the kind of questions that draw us to a theological analysis of the principles behind evangelism. By giving these questions some thought ahead of time, you will be ready to make your contribution to the group discussion.

Evangelizing Sam Revisited

It was more than two years before I mustered up the courage to visit Sam again. Of course he was very gracious and greeted me very warmly once again. At first he did not mention our previous awkward conversation, focusing instead on how I was doing in school and life in general. At one point, he asked me, "What is the best thing that has happened in your life this year?"

I was very reticent about sounding preachy in anything I had to say, but I did want to answer Sam's inquiry honestly. So I told Sam about a small group of guys in my dorm who had developed a habit of getting together for a few minutes every morning before walking to breakfast. There was no agenda for our gathering. We simply made it a point, every morning, to stop in and see what was on our minds for that day. One of us might be dreading an upcoming history test; another might be entangled in a confusing relationship. The things on our minds were sometimes trivial and sometimes weighty. Then, after a few words of encouragement, we would simply pray for one another and be on our way. It was a very simple ten minutes that brought me a strong sense of grounding and support each day.

As I told Sam about this group, it was not my intention to do "evangelism." I was simply answering his question about something meaningful from my life. When I finished, Sam said, "That was one of the most powerful stories of community that I have ever heard. It tells me a lot more about Christianity than that other stuff you brought with you the last time we visited. I'm not kidding, that story really speaks to me."

There was no call for a conversion, no "sinner's prayer," no "Roman Road," and no angry outbursts. It was just an opportunity for me to share something meaningful about my life with someone else. And while I had no intention of practicing evangelism, I think I stumbled across a very authentic and biblical way of doing evangelism that day. That occasion convinced me that there is a way of sharing the joy and justice of the gospel that is not a violation of another person's dignity. We will explore that "more excellent way" together in the forthcoming sessions.

Session Two

The Great Commission and the Initiative of Evangelism

Introduction

I grew up attending a church where the practice of evangelism was a very big part of our understanding of being faithful disciples. Through sermons and lessons we were encouraged to participate ardently in acts of evangelism. A retired police officer in our congregation, Mr. Robinson, took this call very seriously by weekly engagement in what he called "street evangelism." Mr. Robinson had a cache of religious tracts that he would distribute to people filing out of the shipyard at the end of their shift. Sometimes he would be able to strike up conversations, but Mr. Robinson's primary goals were to preach and to get the tracts in people's hands. The tracts were written in a simple, comic book style, with a gripping message. Surely questions like, "If you died today, do you know without any doubt that you would wake up in heaven?" would evoke some kind of reaction out of the person who received the tract, perhaps leading her or him toward an experience of salvation.

It was always interesting to hear Mr. Robinson's stories about his work as a street evangelist and his requests that we pray for the folk whom he had encountered. It was nice to think of someone out there carrying the gospel to people in need. As a child, I had a certain awe and respect for Mr. Robinson's commitment to evangelism. I think a lot of us did. The problem was that Mr. Robinson was always trying to recruit help. And that meant that the rest of us could not just sit in admiration; we had to make a decision for ourselves whether or not we were ready to take up the call to evangelize.

Once, Mr. Robinson successfully recruited my dad to work the street with him. Dad hated it. To my father, the whole experience was simply too intrusive and too confrontational. Yet he gave it a try because he was trying to be faithful to the Great Commission to "go and make disciples." For many years after his sole experience, Dad resisted Mr. Robinson's invitations to go out again in street evangelism. Mr. Robinson's argument was always the same: "But Bob, the Bible tells us to 'go and make disciples.' You won't do that spending your days doing yard work! Come with me and let's 'go.'"

What made Mr. Robinson's argument so compelling is that it resonated perfectly with the church's teachings on evangelism. Despite its compelling resonance, what made Mr. Robinson's argument resistible is that people like my dad could not stomach the reality of accosting others in that way. In other words, even in a church strongly committed to evangelism, the quandary of evangelism was alive and well. While it seemed biblical and right in theory, Mr. Robinson's manner of evangelism was simply too off-putting in practice for many people like my dad. In fact, in all of my years of admiring Mr. Robinson's commitment to evangelism, I only know of two members of our entire church who took up the call to join him more than once.

A Study of Scripture: The Great Commission

In the previous session, I made the argument that the problem with intrusive models of evangelism is not simply a matter of practice, but of principle. In this session, we will address the core biblical issue behind that principle with a crucial question: Is Mr. Robinson's model of evangelism the kind of evangelism envisioned by the Great Commission? As we have seen with the quandary of evangelism in general, the Great Commission itself

seems to be the source, or at least the proof-text, of so many
of the wrong-headed principles and practices of evangelism. For
that reason, we will look closely at the Great Commission, particularly at two versions of that commission that we find in the
Gospels.

Without a doubt, Matthew's version of the Great Commission is the most familiar rendition and is typically what one
refers to by the phrase the Great Commission. However, in
truth, Matthew's version of this commission ought to be called
"A Great Commission," because Luke gives two other rendi-
tions of this commissioning (Luke 24:44–49 and Acts 1:8), with
significant differences. In preparation for the class discussion,
look at the side-by-side comparison of two of these commis-
sions, and see if you can find some of the significant differences
between them.

Matthew's Great Commission	Luke's Great Commission
"Go therefore and make disciples of all nations, baptizing them in the name of the Father and of the Son and of the Holy Spirit, and teaching them to obey everything that I have commanded you." — Matthew 28:19–20a	"But you will receive power when the Holy Spirit has come upon you; and you will be my witnesses in Jerusalem, in all Judea and Samaria, and to the ends of the earth." — Acts 1:8

It is no wonder that Matthew's version of the Great Commission is so popular, because it makes a clear and strong marching
order. It is full of imperatives and active verbs that appeal greatly
to those who are oriented toward action or results: "*Go* and *make*
disciples, *baptizing* them and *teaching* them." One can almost imagine Vince Lombardi pumping his fist and citing this commission
in a locker room pep talk before sending the team running out on
the field. It is also no wonder that Matthew's version of the Great
Commission is often associated with action-oriented events such

as "rallies," competitive language like the slogan to "win the lost at any cost," and even militaristic imagery like "crusades."

Isolating these one and a half verses from Matthew's Gospel as the Great Commission gives the sense that Jesus had completed his earthly sojourn with the disciples and was leaving the rest of the work in their hands. As modern-day disciples, who intend to be faithful to the spirit and calling of the gospel, it seems compelling that one either joins in this action-orientation of the Great Commission or one is unfaithful to the call. The popular reading of Matthew's Great Commission leaves us with only those two choices, it seems. However, this popular reading of Matthew's words is wrong.

To gain a better understanding of the Great Commission, I suggest that we begin with Luke's rendition and then return with fresh perspective to Matthew's words. Luke's version of the Great Commission is less ambiguous than Matthew's because it is harder to isolate the commission and to misread evangelism as primarily a human activity. Instead of imperative and active verbs, Luke uses future verbs with a passive sense:

+ You *will receive* power,

+ when the Holy Spirit *has come* upon you;

+ and you *will be* my witnesses.

With these kinds of verbs, what is primary in Luke's version of the Great Commission is the *receptivity*, not the activity, of the disciples. The commission is to "receive" first, not to "go" first.

What Luke teaches us clearly is that the Great Commission is foremost about Christ's activity and our receptivity. If we take that lesson and return to Matthew's version of the Great Commission, we then notice that the command to "go" is bracketed by two very important statements that Jesus makes regarding himself. Read within these bracketing statements that Matthew gives them, Jesus' words sound quite different than when they are presented as a naked commission.

Jesus came and said to them, "All authority in heaven and on earth has been given to me.

Go, therefore, and make disciples of all nations, baptizing them in the name of the Father and of the Son and of the Holy Spirit, and teaching them to obey everything that I have commanded you.

And remember, I am with you always, to the end of the age."

While isolating the Great Commission makes it sound as if Jesus is done and is leaving it all in our hands, Matthew explicitly recognizes the supremacy of Christ's work and Christ's presence in our acts of going, making disciples, baptizing, and teaching. What Matthew gives us is not simply a marching order; it is a declaration about Christ and Christ's premiere presence within the activity of evangelism. To appeal to the locker room strategy again, it is almost as if the risen Christ is the team on the field and we are the reporters, called to broadcast faithfully what Christ is doing in the world.

The question that confronts any reading of Matthew's Great Commission is, "Who takes the initiative in evangelism, us or Christ?" If the initiative rests with us, as the popular reading of Matthew's Great Commission suggests, then rallies, crusades, and confronting people randomly as they exit the shipyard or as I did Sam are appropriate ways of responding to the Great Commission. But if the initiative of evangelism rests with Christ, as a proper reading of Matthew's commission suggests, then a different kind of faithful response to the commission could be in order.

In response to the question, "Who takes the initiative in evangelism, us or Christ?" a proper reading of Matthew says the same as a plain reading of Luke: the initiative rests with Christ. It is Christ who has all authority; it is Christ who goes with us; it is

Christ who empowers us by the Spirit. While rallies, crusades, and confronting people as they exit the shipyard may be zealous ways to practice evangelism, the key to evangelism is not human effort but Christ's presence and work. All human participation in evangelism is first receptive and always secondly responsive to Christ's initiative. Luke gives us the key to a faithful response to Christ's initiative in evangelism with the word "witness": "You shall be my witnesses."

Hashing It Out: Can I Have a Witness?

One of the unique features of African American and Pentecostal worship services is the "call and response" cadence that one often hears during a sermon. Sometimes a listener will simply nod the head or raise a hand as a sign of agreement. At other times the sign of agreement is much louder or more demonstrative, such as standing up and shouting "Amen!" Sometimes the preacher will solicit the response with the question "Can I have a witness?" It would be every preacher's nightmare to have that question followed by a moment of silence. (That is why I have never ventured to ask for a witness in a Presbyterian church. Rule #1: Know your audience.)

To an outsider, this call and response cadence of worship might seem humorous or odd. But what is happening through this method is that the congregation is not merely listening to a sermon; it is *participating* in it. To be a witness is to participate in the truth of what is being preached. The preacher says, "Weeping may endure for the night, but joy comes in the morning." A congregant says, "Amen," because he is remembering that long, dark period of sleepless tears after the untimely death of a child. He also is giving his assent that while the tears are never too far beneath the surface, there was a special kind of consolation that sustained him during that "dark night of the soul" until he was able to laugh again. It is not just a peculiar tradition at work in this call and response cadence; it is a chance for the congregant to be a witness by participating in the truth of what is being preached.

The participatory nature of African American and Pentecostal worship is a great model for understanding evangelism through Luke's language of being a "witness." As a way of being a witness, evangelism is not, first and foremost, the work that we do. It is our participation in the ongoing presence and work of Christ. In a sermon, the presence and work of Christ is being realized through the reading and proclamation of the gospel. Therefore, the way to be a witness is by nodding one's head, clapping one's hands, standing and shouting "Amen!" or just turning to one's neighbor and saying, "That's been true for my life." The congregation's role is not to preach the sermon itself, but to participate in it.

Outside of a worship service, being a witness is still a matter of participating in the work and presence of Christ by pointing to the truth of the gospel. And that is the essence of evangelism: to be a witness to the redemptive presence of Christ in the world.

Faithful Reflections: The Power of Receptivity

Imagine an evangelism rally at a large stadium. All speeches have been spoken, all songs have been sung, all prayers have been prayed, and now the organizers are preparing for a dramatic moment, when the participants are commissioned as evangelists. The dramatic moment will crescendo to the unfurling of a banner containing the slogan for their evangelism effort. And for that slogan, there are two scenarios.

In the first scenario, the great moment arises, the banner unfurls, and it reads:

Go and Make Disciples!

The crowd goes wild! Instructed by the speakers, energized by the vision, and now commissioned by such clarity of purpose, thousands of enthused evangelists leave the stadium ready to win the world for Christ.

In the second scenario, the great moment arises, the banner unfurls, and it reads:

Wait and Be Filled with Power!

The crowd goes . . . tame.

There just seems to be something lacking about a commission that calls us first and foremost to wait and let Christ take the initiative in evangelism. That explains why Matthew's rendering of the Great Commission, especially if it is isolated from the words that bracket it, is so popular for evangelistic efforts. But to isolate evangelism as the activity of going, making, baptizing, and teaching, apart from the ongoing presence and empowerment of Christ, is to make evangelism into something that it is not.

As long as we view evangelism as an activity in which we take the initiative, intrusive and confrontational practices will be a constant temptation (unless we follow Bishop Spong's advice and abandon the activity of evangelism altogether). If, instead, we view evangelism as an activity where Christ takes the initiative, then the pressure to perform, to persuade, or to measure victories is nullified, because the "success" of evangelism is not up to us. But surely this understanding of being a disciple is too passive, much different than we have been taught to think. Isn't it?

In his introduction to the book *Many Voices, One God*, George Stroup makes an argument regarding missions that interprets well our observations regarding the Great Commission. Stroup says,

> *Too often churches have understood themselves to be taking God to a godless world rather than following God into a world in which God is already redemptively present.*[4]

What we have called Christ's presence and work in the world is exactly what Stroup is referring to by "a world in which God is already redemptively present." What this truth about God, about Christ, and about our world implies for evangelism is that it is practiced with a large dose of humility. We are not primarily goers and doers. We are followers, witnessing and pointing to the one who is primary. And while that humble act of subordinating ourselves to the presence and work of Christ may not be as motivating as a locker room pep talk, it is a familiar way of understanding what it means to be a disciple throughout the New Testament.

In preparation for your class discussion, try to think of some metaphors, imagery, or parables in the New Testament that also emphasize Christ's initiative and our "following," as opposed to our initiative in Christ's absence. Here is one example:

> The popular metaphors of Christ as a shepherd and us as his sheep can be very comforting, particularly in times of grief. They are also striking in their implications. One does not expect a lot out of sheep. They answer the shepherd's call, eat the shepherd's food, and accept the shepherd's nurturing care while they populate and grow wool. To be a sheep is to be primarily receptive and radically dependent on the guidance, intelligence, and protection of the shepherd. In fact, some shepherds suggest that the New Testament metaphor is almost insulting, although that does not seem to be the intention. Nonetheless, the docility and compliance implied in the sheep metaphor is inescapable. Imagine how different it would have been if Christ had said, "I am the good shepherd and you are my sheepdogs!" (I know some folk who seem to think that is exactly what Jesus said!)

Back to Mr. Robinson

So we return to Mr. Robinson, the street evangelist whose attempts to recruit fellow evangelists, even from a strongly evangelistic church, were largely unsuccessful. Is it the case that

Mr. Robinson was faithful to the Great Commission, while the other more reluctant folks were not? A proper reading of Matthew's Great Commission, as well as a plain reading of Luke's version of that commission, would suggest that Mr. Robinson's street evangelism is but one of many faithful responses to Christ's call. The point of the commission is not to induce us to be aggressive or "effective" by many forms of measuring effectiveness. The Great Commission is initially a promise that Christ is with us powerfully in the world, and secondarily a call to be faithful in pointing to the presence and work of Christ in the world. In further sessions we will explore what faithful responses to a present and active Christ can look like.

Evangelism as Conversation: Listening

Introduction

I was teaching Global Studies at the University of Iowa, when one of my students, "John," began dropping by my office to discuss his grades and work. His grades were not going well. He was such a passionate advocate for environmental causes that he put things like term papers, studying for tests, and so forth on a back burner. It turned out that while I was concerned about his grade in my class, he was doing better in my class than any of his other classes! So in the course of our conversations we talked about priorities, budgeting time, harnessing passion with reason, and other things that I hoped would be helpful to him as a student and an advocate.

Not long into our conversations, John asked me a surprising question: "How can you be a Christian minister and still care about global issues and the environment?" My impulsive reaction was to get defensive about the assumptions behind this question and argue that it is entirely reasonable for one to be a person of faith and passionate about God's world. But John's question was sincere. So I bit my tongue and searched for a way to explore his question. It is a good thing that I did.

What grew out of John's question was a chance for me to listen to his story. Raised in a devoutly Christian home, attending a church where his own doubts and questions were not particularly welcomed, John was not only suspicious of all things Christian, he was also estranged from his parents because of that suspicion.

They saw him as someone who had strayed from the true faith and whose separation from God was the source of their disagreements. He saw them as slavishly adhering to a faith tradition that squelches dissent and rationalizes despoiling the same environment that he worked so hard to protect. The assumptions behind John's loaded question to me were assumptions that he had come by painfully.

Thank God I did not react defensively when John asked a question that I had every right to challenge. Instead, as I listened to his story, John and I found a lot of common ground, beginning with our shared critique of representations of Christianity that ignore the harmful effects of human actions on the environment. Along the way, I learned a lot by listening to John's critique of Christianity. Quite frankly, John's rationale for his grievances with the church was one of the best lessons in environmental stewardship that I had ever heard.

The conversations that I had with John were true conversations, where we found ourselves agreeing with one another in unexpected places, disagreeing at times, but most often helping each other to move to better understandings and opinions. A real pivotal moment was when I asked John to help me to understand what made him so passionate about the environment, even to the point of almost flunking out of college. To this core question, John struggled for the right words. He would not say, "Preserving the earth is important so that humans can exist." That was the kind of human-centered answer that he thought the church and his political opponents perpetuated too much. He wanted to say that there was something inherently good and value-filled about the earth that was greater than its service to human needs or wants.

In the end, John and I found the language that he was looking for in the first creation story in the Bible, where God creates the world and pronounces it "good" even before humanity is created. That discovery was a huge breakthrough for John. When our conversations began, the word "God" was laden with lots of negative images in John's mind, and he saw "creation" as a code word for ideas that were unscientific and ideological. But through our conversations John discovered something about God that he intuitively already lived by: God is the creator who pronounces the earth "good" in a cosmic, eternally significant way.

For the first time in many years, John willingly embraced the God of the scriptures. It was not an "evangelism encounter" in the sense that John was kneeling on my office floor, saying the sinner's prayer. It was not a "Campus Crusade" moment, when John was converted to Christianity because I outwitted all arguments to the contrary. It was simply that in the course of our conversation John found a point of contact between his deepest passion and the biblical revelation of God as creator. In other words, after a long time of rejecting it, John "came to himself" by rediscovering the revelation of God in the scriptures.

Setting the Stage: Beginning Principles for Evangelism

I have argued that the problem with most models of evangelism is not a problem of practice, but a problem of principle. To this point, we have established two working principles for evangelism that challenge previous models. In session 1, we critiqued the "first step" in the "Roman Road to Salvation," which begins every person's story with the scripture passage "All have sinned and fall short of the glory of God." As true as that verse may be, it is *not* truly a "first word" of anyone's life. If, following Paul Tillich, we identify human sinfulness as "estrangement," then the first word about any life is not that one is fallen, but that one originally belongs to God. Therefore, our first principle for evangelism is this:

+ **Originally and primarily, each one belongs to God.**

In session 2 we saw that the Great Commission is not primarily about our "going" and "doing." It is the presence and work of Christ that is primary in evangelism, and we are called as "witnesses" to that presence and work. Or, to use George Stroup's

terminology, we point to a world where God is already redemptively present. Therefore, our second principle for evangelism
is this:

* **The redemptive presence and work of Christ goes before us.**

In this session we will explore a way of practicing evangelism
that honors both of these principles. So we ask: What would the
practice of evangelism look like if we addressed people, not primarily as fallen sinners, but primarily as children of God, however
estranged? Likewise, what would the practice of evangelism look
like if we assumed that, instead of our bringing Christ to every person and place, Christ's work and presence is always ahead of us?
In contrast to many popular models of evangelism, an evangelism
that follows these two principles would necessarily take the shape
of a conversation as opposed to an argument or a monologue.

Hashing It Out: Evangelism as a Dialogue

Most models of evangelism, such as the model at work in my ill-
fated attempt to save Sam in session 1, are built on the premises
of a monologue. The most egregious form of this monological
model would be the street preacher, just hammering away at the
gates of hell on behalf of whoever happens to walk by. But even
within a friendlier context of what looks a dialogue — whether
encountering a stranger in the mall or chatting with a friend over
coffee — most models of evangelism are essentially monologues.
We can describe the dynamics of evangelism monologues in terms
of the "The I-You Components."

The I-You Components

I...	You...
am a child of God	are lost in sin
have experienced grace	are under judgment
know the truth	are living a lie
need to help you	need to become like me

Of course, it is rare that a model for evangelism would encourage anyone to put these dynamics on the table as nakedly as I have described them. But these are precisely the dynamics at work in most models of evangelism. Even in friendly models that encourage "dialogue" as the means of evangelism, the agenda at work is essentially a monologue: the evangelist has the message and whatever conversation takes place is simply the occasion for sharing that message.

One example of this kind of monologue posing as a dialogue is found in a book called *Evangelism Made Slightly Less Difficult*, by Nick Pollard. Pollard describes a process for evangelism that he calls "positive deconstruction," which he explains like this:

> The process of positive deconstruction recognizes and affirms the elements of truth to which individuals already hold, but it also helps them discover for themselves the inadequacies of the underlying worldviews that they have absorbed. The aim is to awaken a heart response that says, "I am not so sure that what I believe is right after all. I want to find out more about Jesus." At last they are taking their first steps along the road toward faith in Christ.[5]

While Pollard's process of "positive deconstruction" is premised on conversation, it is a conversation with a decided working agenda. Particularly, the role of "listening" in the conversation is a specific kind of strategic listening, listening for an opening to counter the other's story with what Pollard calls "the Christian worldview." We can describe "listening" in Pollard's model as:

+ Identifying the worldview

+ Analyzing the worldview

+ Affirming the "elements of truth" in the worldview

+ Discovering the error of the worldview

Once the error of the other's worldview is discovered then the other person moves into a crisis of faith that the gospel can address.

There is a lot that I find commendable about Pollard's process of evangelism. It is certainly a vast improvement over my awkward attempt to convert Sam! But in principle Pollard's process is still a monologue, no matter how conversational it might appear. Especially telling is that in Pollard's process all of the "I-You Components" are intact. No matter what the other person has to say, even if she should happen to embrace some commendable "elements of truth," the dynamics underlying the conversation are: You are lost, you are under judgment, you are living a lie, you need to become like me. As long as these dynamics lie hidden beneath the veneer of conversation, there is not genuine listening or genuine dialogue.

If we follow our two principles — "Originally and primarily, each one belongs to God" and "The redemptive presence and work of Christ goes before us" — a whole new world of genuine dialogue opens up for evangelism. The ultimate difference is that, with our principles at work, everyone's story has real and meaningful significance; it is not just a jumping off point for our monologue. With these two principles at work, everyone's story is a "faith journey" in some way, no matter how angry, confused, or destructive that journey might be. And, with these two principles at work, everyone's story deserves our genuine listening because Christ is already actively present in their life ahead of us.

John's story was a faith journey that included a rejection of the church of his birth. It would have been easy to consider his story as just one big mistake, premised on a lie with only a few "elements of truth" mixed in. My impression was that his parents and the church of his childhood saw his story that way. But John's story was a story of courage and passion, a story of love for the earth and for life. More important, since John is originally and primarily a beloved child of God and the redemptive presence and work of Christ is already in John's life, John's story was a significant faith journey and not just a set-up for my message. Indeed, I am a better steward of the environment today because John's story was a story through which I was changed and enlightened.

A Beginning Scripture:
The Prodigal Who "Comes to Himself"

The question arises, of course, that if the conversations of evangelism are not strategically structured toward uncovering the other's need for Christ, then what are they about? After all, the Great Commission itself has an agenda. It says to go and "make disciples," not just to go and "have some really interesting conversations." So if we are not listening for a weakness, an error, or some other sort of opening for sharing the Christian message in someone's life, what are we listening for?

The Great Commission does indeed have an agenda, and we are called to follow it. But it is a commission that is wrapped in a promise. Therefore, our practice of evangelism is as attentive to the promise as to the commission. In order to follow a commission that emphasizes first the presence and work of Christ, then the *first* thing that evangelism listens for is the work and presence of Christ in another person's life. We do not simply listen for "elements of truth" that someone has fortunately embraced along with the errors of their worldview. We are listening for visitations of grace, the evidence that Christ is already redemptively present in someone's life. Those visitations of grace might come in expressions of rejection; they might appear in small victories or stories of compassion. But if we believe in the promise that wraps the commission, the first thing we listen for is the redemptive work and presence of Christ in someone's life.

There was a significant moment in my conversations with John when John discovered the foundation for his passion for the earth in the creative God of the scriptures. That moment was a beautiful, pivotal moment in John's life, which is reminiscent of a critical turning point in the well-known story of the Prodigal Son

(Luke 15). As Jesus tells the story, the young man had wandered far from home, squandering the inheritance money that he had demanded from his father. When he had spent everything, a severe famine hit the region, so the young man was desperate for work and took a job feeding pigs. Here is how Jesus describes the turning point for the young man's journey:

> He would gladly have filled himself with the pods that the pigs were eating; and no one gave him anything. But *when he came to himself,* he said, "How many of my father's hired hands have bread enough and to spare, but here I am dying of hunger!"

It is this moment of "coming to himself" that I witnessed in John's experience. After a long time of walking away from the faith of his childhood, John "came to himself" by finding his own passion in one of the oldest theological commitments of the Judeo-Christian tradition: the understanding of God as the creator and sustainer of the world. To be sure, there are critical differences between John's story and the story of the Prodigal Son. But it was a vivid experience when John "came to himself" by rediscovering the doctrine of creation, not as a scientific argument, but as a way of expressing his wonder and reverence for the earth.

Beyond the "I-You Components" to "Godly Presumptions"

When it comes to the "listening" side of the conversation of evangelism, it is these kinds of moments, when one is "coming to oneself" that we should listen for. Nick Pollard is probably correct in assuming that many of us embrace a mixture of "elements of truth" and "errors in our worldview." But to structure our dialogue as a way of uncovering the errors is to follow the "I-You Components" of monological evangelism. If we follow our two principles — "Originally and primarily, each one belongs to God" and "The redemptive presence and work of Christ goes before us" — we enter our conversations in a different way. We begin with what I want to call "Godly Presumptions." We presume:

+ that our conversational partner is a beloved child of God,
+ that God is already redemptively present in her life. And, therefore,
+ that her noblest and best moments are blessings from God, and
+ that her weakest or angriest moments are occasions for God's grace.

As it turns out, with godly presumptions we make the same presumptions about others that we make about ourselves! We can make these godly presumptions about everyone we meet, not because humans are all stamped alike, but because God is faithful to all alike. With these godly presumptions in place, the dynamics of a genuine evangelism conversation are not "I have the truth" and "You are lost in sin." Rather, because of God's grace in our lives, a genuine evangelism conversation rests on the assumption that each person has something significant to say.

The biggest difference between genuine conversation and the kind of monologues that most models of evangelism embrace is that when we assume that God is already redemptively present in someone's life, we can really listen to that person's story, and not just listen for a strategic occasion for sharing our message. The other difference is that when we embrace these godly presumptions and engage in genuine conversations, *every* conversation becomes an occasion for evangelism, and not just the conversations where we have a strategic outcome in mind.

Session Four

Listening and Telling

"Tata Jesus Is Bängala!"

Barbara Kingsolver's wonderful novel *The Poisonwood Bible* is a story about a Baptist missionary, his wife, and their four daughters as they live and work in the Congo.[6] The missionary of the novel has no lack of zeal; he is determined to baptize every person in the Congo into the Christian faith. However, one of the missionary's many problems with his attempts at evangelization is that he has no respect for the wisdom of the Congolese and therefore does not bother trying to learn the culture into which he has immersed himself and his family. That failure is especially evident when the missionary tries to circumvent his translator and speak directly to the Congolese in their language, Kikongo, the subtlety of which he completely misunderstands.

At the end of each sermon the father tries to say something equivalent to "Jesus is Lord!" with the cry, "Tata Jesus is Bängala!" "Bängala" means something precious and sweet, but only if it is said correctly. What the father fails to learn is that in the village's dialect, most words can mean several things, depending on the inflection and gesture that one uses. It happens that, "Bängala" is also the word that describes "poisonwood," a kind of noxious tree that affects the skin like a very strong poison ivy and, if one should mistakenly burn the wood in a fire, can sicken the household with the fumes.

According to the Baptist missionary's insightful daughter Adah, the way that the missionary would say "Tata Jesus is Bängala!" at the end of each sermon, suggested that he meant something like,

"Praise the Lord, hallelujah, my friends! For Jesus will make you itch like nobody's business."[7] Small wonder, then, that the father's sermons always leave his listeners looking puzzled and not at all inclined to meet this Jesus whom he has so vividly described.

One wonders how many of us, working not in a distant context, but in our own places and with the best of intentions, have, nevertheless, presented the gospel as if we were saying "Tata Jesus is Bängala!" I know that I almost made this error once in a completely innocent way.

While I was a student in seminary, the chaplain at a local correctional school for girls asked me to preach in her absence on several occasions. The chaplain was a very thoughtful woman, who wisely asked me about what I was preparing to say in my first visit to their chapel. At the heart of my sermon was a story about my father and a corresponding connection to how God loves us as a loving father.

The metaphor of God as father is certainly biblical, and the story of my experience with my own father was as adequate as human analogies of God can be. But the chaplain offered this word of caution. More than 95 percent of the girls who entered their correctional program had experienced some sort of sexual abuse by a father or a father figure. Despite the biblical use of the metaphor of "father," despite the meaning that such a metaphor held for me personally, it carried an entirely different meaning for many of these girls. Their common story made the metaphor of father a tragic metaphor, which actually miscommunicated the very message that I intended to proclaim. In effect, I was preparing to get up and declare, "Tata Jesus is Bängala!"

In the previous session, we considered "listening" as an essential part of the conversation of evangelism. Rather than strategic listening, which listens to the other's story only as a pretext for beginning our monologue, genuine listening is built on the premise that the other's story is meaningful. The theological guarantee of that meaningfulness is nothing less than God's redemptive presence in the world.

In this session, we will consider the critical connection between listening and telling. As opposed to a model of evangelism that fixes the Christian message into a "one size fits all" kind of pattern, we will explore how important listening is for telling the good news of the gospel effectively — even truthfully. Without listening, we could easily set out to say something wonderful, but in fact be saying something like, "Tata Jesus is Bängala!"

Scripture Study: Paul's Experience in Athens (Acts 17:16–34)

The story of Paul's missionary venture into Athens is an excellent example of listening-as-a-means-of-speaking-effectively. Athens was a city still basking in the afterglow of its reputation as an intellectual center for Epicurean and Stoic philosophy. It was also a place where idols of many sorts were readily visible. As such, Athens represents a stark picture of the gospel's encounter with numerous alien belief systems. One would think that Athens would be just the kind of place that would ignite an evangelist like Paul, causing him to launch into a diatribe against the foolishness of idolatry, the emptiness of philosophy, and so forth. However, while Paul has no doubts about the wrongness of idolatry, his reaction is quite different than one might expect.

I need to pause here and point out something related to this scripture text and some of the interpretive issues surrounding the act of translating the scriptures from their original language into one's own language. Sometimes the theology of the translator will affect the translation of the scriptures. For this text, one's view of other belief systems may affect the translation of certain key terms. For example, the King James Version translates the opening line of Paul's sermon as, "Ye men of Athens, I perceive that in all things ye are too superstitious" (Acts 17:22). With this translation, the King James Version interprets Paul's sermon as confrontational from the very beginning. Other translations, however, start off

Paul's sermon quite differently. The New Revised Standard Version translates this sentence as, "Athenians, I see how extremely religious you are in every way." The difference between "too superstitious" and "extremely religious" is rather striking. Either translation is technically plausible, since languages do not have simple one-to-one correspondence. Therefore, what seems to be the deciding factor in cases like this is the theology that the translator brings to the text. If one assumes that Paul must be confrontational with the Athenians, the KJV translation is more appealing. If one does not assume confrontation, the NRSV translation is more appealing. Either way, there is no explicit *biblical* or *literary* reason for choosing between "too superstitious" or "extremely religious." The reasons are more theological.

At issue in the translation of Paul's sermon is a concern for the integrity of the Christian message. Quite often, it seems that evangelism operates under the assumption that if one honors rather than disparages the truth or the genuine religious quest of another belief system, then one is "watering down" the gospel in order to make it more palatable to others. That is why so many approaches to evangelism insist on a rigid, dogmatic approach to faith that excludes any possibility of genuine listening because belief systems other than Christianity are simply wrong. The simplicity and rigidity of the "Roman Road to Salvation" lends itself to this kind of dogmatism.

I raise this issue because I want to invite you to read this encounter between Paul and the Athenians in a fresh and promising way. My interpretation will vary from some translations of this text, because I am consciously choosing a more open theological lens through which to read this story.[8] Namely, I invite you to consider this event as exemplary of *genuine listening* in the activity of evangelism. We hear Paul's voice predominantly in this story, but through Paul's comments we will see how important genuine listening is to sharing the gospel.

1. Paul begins by noting that the Athenians are extremely religious.

It would be easy to assume that Paul is just making nice when he calls the Athenians "extremely religious." But, in fact, Paul tells the Athenians that he went through their city and looked carefully at the objects of their worship. So now we wonder whether this means that Paul was busy shaking his head at the Athenians' wrongheaded faith or if he was seeing promising signs of genuine searching behind their manufacturing of and dedication to idols.

2. One altar in particular provides Paul with an opportunity to share the gospel.

While observing the Athenians' object and relics, Paul found among them an altar with the inscription, "To an unknown god." For Paul, this was an opportunity to share his own faith, beginning with the words, "What therefore you worship as unknown, this I proclaim to you." It is important to note that Paul begins his presentation of the Christian message at the place where he perceives the Athenians' interest is.

3. Paul presents a bold and faithful message of God's grace.

In contrast to the gods portrayed by idols, Paul proclaims the God who is Lord of heaven and of earth, who does not live in shrines created by human hands. Nor does this God need anything because this God is the one who gives life and breath to all that is mortal. God's absolute self-sufficiency is not compatible with the kind of piety that Paul perceived in the proliferation of idols and shrines in Athens. Rather than simply "making nice" or watering down the gospel, Paul is willing to point out the differences between his own message and the piety of the Athenians.

To this point, everything we have observed in Paul's encounter with the Athenians is rather common in many models of evangelism and missions. One could even argue that Paul is demonstrating the "positive deconstruction" that we addressed in the last session. But the next two observations will separate Paul's way of evangelizing from any model that does not engage in genuine listening.

4. Paul's message of God's grace *includes* the Athenians' own expressions of piety.

Paul's message is a bold and faithful proclamation, not a watered-down gospel at all. In effect, Paul proclaims the resurrection of the Christ as God's assurance that God will judge the world righteously. Nonetheless, Paul's message is not simply an exclusive "counterpoint" to the Athenians' belief systems. In fact, Paul quotes some of their own thinkers to make his point. In one case, Paul explicitly refers to their tradition saying, "As even some of your own poets have said, 'For we too are his offspring'" (Acts 17:28b). In another case, Paul cites one of their thinkers without making the reference explicit. Perhaps Paul's lack of a citation would explain why a quote from a pagan poet has become one of the most memorable and beloved quotations from the Acts of the Apostles for Christian piety: "In [God] we live and move and have our being" (v. 28a).

It is important to recognize that Paul quotes these poets approvingly, not as a foil, not as a springboard to his counterpoint, and not as a way of showing the Athenians the errors of their worldview. Rather than simply listening strategically, Paul was genuinely listening. Idolatrous though they may be, there was some pretty darn good theology wrapped up in the Athenians' piety. And Paul appreciates it.

5. Paul finds greater expression of his own faith as a result of genuine listening.

Finally, here is the part of genuine listening that is most challenging and rewarding to the evangelist. Paul found among the Athenians a search for faith that allowed him to consider and express his own belief in the gospel in fresh and creative ways.

That is to say, Paul's encounter with the Athenians was more than a point of common ground; it was an occasion for growth on his part. It is in this sermon that Paul articulates a view of the world that is generously expansive and inclusive of many searches for faith. Paul says, "From one ancestor God made all nations to inhabit the whole earth, and God allotted the times of their existence and the boundaries of the places where they would live, so that they would search for God and perhaps grope for God and find God — though indeed God is not far from each one of us" (vv. 26–27). What an amazingly abundant view of God and God's capacious love for humanity!

I had a Church History and Missions professor in seminary who once told me that being in a loving relationship with people of other faiths was more instrumental in strengthening his Christian faith than anything else he had ever done. The same can be said for many relationships. A Buddhist neighbor can teach us the profound meaning of Jesus' prayer that his followers can "become one" in John 17. A student who rages at the church's compliance in despoiling the environment can teach us volumes about the doctrine of creation. A girl's tragic experience with a father figure can encourage us to look beyond the metaphor of God as "father" for expansive metaphors of understanding God's relationship with us. A neighbor whose faith in God has never recovered from the loss of a child can direct us to those difficult lament psalms that cry out, "My God, my God, why have you forsaken me?" (Psalm 22).

Paul's encounter with the Athenians — pagan idol worshipers though they might have been — helped to expand his own view of God's amazing grace. As a result of his genuine listening, Paul found a bold and positive way to proclaim his faith in the God who comes to us through Jesus Christ. This is not a "watered down" moment, when Paul compromises the gospel. On the contrary, it is a moment when Paul finds new, vivid expression for his faith. And we know why! It is because God was always already redemptively present among the Athenians that Paul is able to be a witness to Jesus Christ while discovering, celebrating, and learning from what God has already done among the Athenians.

Faithful Reflections:
An Outline for a Theology of Evangelism

The theologian Doug Ottati has written powerfully that the theology on which the Christian faith is built should be "capacious, generous, and open rather than narrow, stingy, and closed."[9] It takes precisely a "capacious, generous, and open" theology to engage in genuine listening as a part of evangelism. Here we can sketch out what that kind of theology might look like.

1. God's ways are higher than our ways.

Many times when theologians run out of explanations, they use this phrase from Isaiah — "God's ways are higher than our ways" — as a fallback provision. For the great Reformed theologian John Calvin, however, the distance between God's thoughts and human thoughts was not a fallback provision. It is a constitutive principle for all of theology. Calvin argued that God, in God's essence, is unknowable to humanity. Therefore, anything that we might presume to know about God is only knowable insofar as God "accommodates" Godself to human understanding.[10] Hence, one could argue that whatever we "know" about God is, at best, our frail and human attempt to capture that which ultimately lies beyond human knowledge.

Calvin's point is that when we speak of knowing God or even of receiving a "revelation" of God, it is not because we have elevated ourselves to knowing the heights of glory. It is possible only because God accommodates Godself to the lowliness of human finitude. For a theology of evangelism, the implication of knowing that God's ways are higher than our ways is that we have a built-in disposition of humility in every expression of the gospel. Because God is too wonderful for us, we have the humility of knowing that what we believe and how we express our faith is always necessarily inadequate to the greatness and glory of God.

2. In Christ, God is made known to us.

The ultimate act of God "accommodating" Godself to us is contained in the ancient Christian profession "God was in Christ." In Christ, all that is distant between us and God is overcome. In Christ, God has become knowable, not as a distant "other," but as one of us. In Christ, we have access to knowing God. That is not to say that, in Christ, we have some kind of mystical insight that elevates us beyond human finitude. Rather, it works in the other direction. The Apostle Paul describes so well in Philippians 2:5–11 that Christ "lowered" himself, even to the point of hanging on the cross.

So while we have the humility of knowing that God's ways are higher than our ways, we also have the confidence that, in Christ, God has come to us in a knowable, relational way. Therefore, our humility is transformed into a *humble confidence*. It is not the kind of humility that shuts our mouths and leaves us without a message. It is a humble confidence that even though our expressions of faith are always necessarily inadequate to the greatness and glory of God, it is sufficient because, in Christ, God has come to us.

3. In Christ, God is always already redemptively present in the world.

I introduced this principle in the last session, so now it is time to place it within our theology for evangelism. To say that, in Christ, God is always already redemptively present in the world is to remind ourselves that the incarnation of Christ is not merely a historical event. Perhaps William Stacy Johnson expressed it best when he said, "The incarnation was not a thirty-three-year experiment but the permanent mode of God's engagement to save."[11]

As we saw in session 2, the presence of Christ is an essential part of the Great Commission. It is also that part of our theology of evangelism that enables us to exercise genuine listening. Because Christ is always already redemptively present in people's lives, even before we arrive bearing our message, we can listen to their stories, their experiences, their beliefs, and even their doubts *as one way of listening for what God is doing in the world.*

Tata Jesus Is Bängala?

Evangelism is poorly served whenever zealous evangelists venture out into the world without listening. Despite the best of intentions, without listening the effect of our message could be something like "Tata Jesus is Bängala!" Therefore, any model of evangelism that is narrow, stingy, or closed in its theology runs the risk of miscommunicating the good news of the gospel. A theology of evangelism that is capacious, generous, and open is much more in harmony with the way that God has graciously accommodated to us in Christ. Because God's ways are higher than our ways, because God was in Christ, because in Christ God is always already redemptively present in the world, we have a disposition of humble confidence, which invites us to genuinely listen to the experiences of others.

Session Five

Telling Stories Faithfully

Kazuo Ishiguro is a profound storyteller. What is distinct about his storytelling is how he can change the entire meaning of one story by situating it within a larger story. In his book *The Remains of the Day*, Ishiguro tells the story of a manservant serving in a large manor house in England.[12] The manservant is the narrator, so the slow, deliberate cadence of the narration demonstrates the meticulous attention to perfecting the smallest detail that makes the manservant excel at his craft. His focus, his dedication, and his devotion to assuring that everything is in order for his master and the master's guests are what make the manservant the epitome of what is sometimes called the "Protestant work ethic." Being a manservant is not just his job; it is his entire way of being. One cannot but admire the manservant's work ethic.

However, through a series of flashbacks and present time narratives, it slowly becomes apparent that there is something wrong here. The readers, along with the manservant, begin to notice some peculiarities about the parties that the manservant is maintaining so scrupulously. The master, it turns out, is a sympathizer of the Nazi regime in Germany, and his soirées are attempts to drum up more support among other wealthy Englishmen. Once we learn of the master's interests, the manservant's devotion to his job changes from being admirable to being problematic. His attention to detail now has a horrifying quality to it, because of the larger purpose that the master's parties are serving.

What Kazuo Ishiguro demonstrates is how our personal stories take on new significance when we place them within larger contextualizing stories.[13] Admittedly, the example I have drawn from *The Remains of the Day* is a negative one. It shows how a personal story of dedication can turn to a tragic story by situating it within a horrific event like the agenda of the Nazi regime. But the alternative is possible also. The details of one's personal story can demonstrate pain, tragedy, or heartache. But when placed within the larger story of God's redemption, the meaning and relevance of that same story change dramatically.

At the heart of evangelism is the *evangel*, which literally means the "good news." There is news to share in evangelism, a story to be told. For evangelism, we tell our personal story within the larger story of God's redemptive presence in the world. In addition, a listening evangelism, as we have described genuine listening throughout this book, offers an invitation as well. In addition to sharing our stories, we solicit the stories of others. Within that dialogue, we invite others to find greater meaning of their personal story within the larger story of God's redemptive presence as well.

Our purpose in this session is to find ways to tell our stories that are faithful to the gospel, authentic to our experience, and mindful of the expansive nature of God's love. We will begin by looking at how storytelling is a dynamic process, using an insight that we gain from therapeutic counseling. From there we will look at the components that comprise faithful stories that are both authentic to our lives and expressive of God's capacious love. In the end, our hope is that telling our stories can be a wonderful, fulfilling way of sharing the joy and justice of the gospel.

Dynamic Storytelling

There is an important change taking place in therapeutic practices that can be very instructive for the practice of evangelism. The common image of therapy is that of the patient reclining on a couch spilling his story while the expert therapist listens. After the cleansing experience of telling one's story, the patient turns to the expert therapist for her insight into what is truly going on and her wise counsel for how to make it better. It is a model that reflects the medical procedure of examination, diagnosis, and cure.

Frankly, therapists have often dreaded that moment when the client looks at them and expects the word that unlocks the problems of their life. It is not that simple. And increasingly we are realizing that this common image of therapy expects too much wisdom out of the therapist and not enough from within the client. In fact it is often the client who holds within her the key that begins to unlock her problem.

One way of moving beyond the shortcomings of the common image of therapy is an approach called "narrative (or story) therapy." Kelly Walker-Jones and Dick Hester explain the difference this way:

> Unlike conventional therapy, which views the therapist as the expert healer, narrative therapy views the client as the expert on his or her own life. The therapist, in turn, becomes a curious listener who never assumes to know things ahead of the client. Instead, the narrative therapist works side-by-side with client. Together, they become "archeologists of hope" who are unearthing untold stories.[14]

Narrative therapy begins with inviting the patient to tell his story, but it doesn't stop there. The beauty of storytelling is that it is a dynamic process: Stories can be told and retold in many ways. My story might originally be the expression of a tragedy that has caused enormous harm to my life. In that story, I might see myself primarily, or perhaps even solely, as a victim. As such, there is enormous value in simply expressing the pain of my story. But my story can also be told in a different way. It may take time and encouraging companionship, but my story can also be told as a story of how I have survived that tragedy, however broken. In narrative therapy, the therapist's role would be to listen well in order to provide an appropriate wider set of images and vocabulary for renewing my story. Then, my story can remain authentic to the tragedy that I have experienced *and* be transformed into a story with new possibilities and hope.

Walker-Jones and Hester borrow the phrase "archeology of hope" to point to possibilities of uncovering a new story beneath an old story.[15] They explain that in their faith-based practice this possibility is predicated on God's redemptive presence in the world:

> Theologically, our project is grounded in the belief that God is constantly at work in the world, even when we cannot see it. Narrative work takes a position of relentless optimism, believing there is always another story that may disclose God's work and invitation.[16]

The possibilities for adapting the practices of narrative therapy in evangelism are obvious. As evangelists, rather than adopting the position of the expert, we adopt the position of a companion. Through genuine listening, we solicit the story of others, under the conviction that God is already redemptively present in their lives. Therefore, their story does not need to fit into a proper formula, any specific theology, or any religious language, because their story is not up for our judgment. It is not our job to "deconstruct" their story, as Nick Pollard suggests in his method of evangelism (see session 3). As a companion, we solicit and listen sympathetically to the other's story — even if it is an angry story, like that of my student John and his rejection of his childhood faith.

But narrative therapy does not end with listening to another's story and neither does evangelism. In addition to genuine listening, evangelism is also a matter of storytelling. By telling our stories, we offer a way for the others to reconceptualize their story. In my conversations with John, he found a better, more authentic vocabulary for his passion for the environment when I directed him to the creation story in the first chapter of Genesis. As with Kazuo Ishiguro's novel, John's personal story of passion for the environment took on new meaning and form when we situated it within the larger story of how God created the world and called it good.

As evangelists, we are not called to be therapists in the strict sense of the term, but we are indeed called to be companions in every sense of that term. However, for many folks, the part of evangelism that involves inviting and genuinely listening to another person's story comes rather easily. It is the other side of this conversational companionship that poses the problem — the role of telling our own story. It is to that side of the conversation that we will now turn.

Living in a Three-Storied Universe

I suggest that, despite the vindication of Galileo, the revolution of Copernicus, and the voyage of Columbus, the ancients were correct to say that we live in a "three-storied universe."[17] Only it is not three-storied in the *spatial* sense of the heavens above, the earth between, and the underworld below. It is three-storied in the *experiential* sense that faithful evangelism tells three types of inter-related stories, each of which is incomplete until it is connected to the other two.

The components of this three-storied experience are built around Jesus' answer to a question inquiring about the point of human life. A lawyer asked, "Teacher, which commandment in the law is the greatest?" Jesus' answer is what we have called throughout this book "The Great Commandment":

> "You shall love the Lord your God with all your heart, and with all your soul, and with all your mind." This is the first and greatest commandment. And the second is like it: "You shall love your neighbor as yourself." (Matthew 22:37–40)

The three objects of love in Jesus' answer are God, neighbor, and self. Likewise, the three interrelated stories in telling the good news of the gospel are stories of God, our neighbor, and ourselves: God's story, my neighbor's story, and my story.

"God's story" tells the story of God's redemptive presence in the world. "My neighbor's story" tells the story of how God's redemptive presence includes my neighbors in the widest sense of the word, from the totality of all creation to the person sitting across the table from me. And "my story" is the story of the way that God's redemptive presence has shaped and changed my own life. The key to faithful storytelling is not to isolate any one of these stories, but to keep all three of these components in view so that they shape one another. We will look at each of these components separately first and then consider them together as an interrelated story.

"God's Story":
God's Redemptive Presence in the World

It is intimidating to try to tell "God's story." It is a huge story. According to the Christian tradition, it is a story that is hinted at through nature, supposed through reason, revealed in the scriptures, and incarnate in Jesus Christ. Try telling that in fifty words or less! It cannot be done, even with endless words. Perhaps that is why John, the Gospel writer, ends his story with this very humble disclaimer: "But there are many other things that Jesus did; if every one of them were written down, I suppose that the world itself could not contain the books that would be written" (John 21:25).

John's humble disclaimer encourages us to remember that *any* telling of "God's story" cannot be perfect or complete. Every human attempt to tell "God's story" inevitably falls short of fully capturing the truth. So relax. What we want to capture is a simple plot that runs through the complexity of the details. Therefore, I suggest that we think of "God's story" as having a basic three-part plot.

- God is faithful
- We are not
- God loves us anyway

Not every story can be pegged easily into this scheme, but the momentum of the stories seems to fit it well. Time and time again God is faithful, God's people prove unfaithful, and God loves anyway. While this story line is simple, it is told in many rich details throughout the scriptures:

- God creates Adam and Eve; they disobey; God is merciful to them by giving them work and family.

- Adam and Eve have children; the older one kills the younger one; God spares him with mercy.

- God rescues the people of Israel from slavery in Egypt; they complain against God; God gives them water from a rock and manna from the skies.

For the Christian community, the story of Christ certainly fits this scheme:

- Christ comes to humanity as a gift from God; humanity puts Christ to death; God raises Christ up as our salvation.

Theologically, this simple plot reminds us that "God's story" is primarily a story of God's initiative, not human achievement. As such, this simple plot is a *counterstory* to what might be the most popular theology in America: "If I am good enough, God will love me." We hear *that* story — a story where God responds to our initiative, not a story of God's initiative — in jokes, in throwaway comments, as well as in anxieties, testimonies, and even in a lot of sermons. We heard it in the Roman Road to Salvation in session 1, which begins with *our* fallenness and turns on *our* activity, only after which does God respond by saving us.

Our plot line — God is faithful; we are not; God loves us anyway — is a protest against this popular theology. "God's story" begins with God's initiative and puts the promise and hope of salvation on God, rather than on us. As such, it is true to the biblical claims of God's faithfulness and human fickleness. It helps us to understand the importance of the Psalm refrain: "God's steadfast love endures forever."

Our plot reflects this refrain from the Psalms by saying that, in addition to God's faithfulness and our unfaithfulness, "God loves us anyway." Without this final, steadfast love, "God's story" would be a tragic story ending in human failure and God's judgment. Instead, "God's Story" says "God is faithful; we are not; God loves us anyway." It is a simple plot line that puts the initiative and final word with God, where they belong.

My Neighbor's Story:
God's Redemptive Presence Writ Large

The second component of our three-storied experience is the part that is missing in too many models of evangelism. "My neighbor's story" is a critical component for two reasons. First, including "my neighbor's story" in our complex of stories prevents reductive storytelling, or storytelling that only tells a fraction of the whole story. Reductive storytelling in evangelism is the unfortunate result of overemphasizing "personal salvation." To be sure, it is God's gift to us that we are invited to appropriate God's grace for ourselves. As such, salvation is indeed a moment of wonder that touches us at the deepest and most personal level. However, when we express this personal connection that we have to God's story of redemption, we risk reducing God's embrace of *all* creation, Christ's death on behalf of *all* humanity, to *what's in it for me.*

I sincerely believe that people who express their faith experience with very personal language do not intend to reduce the gospel as dramatically as it might sound. A pastor friend of mine insists that he once heard someone claim, "When Jesus was hanging on the cross, he was thinking of me." Unfortunately, like this claim, a lot of what passes for "personal testimony" appears to leave "my neighbor's story" out of the picture.

Even if those who speak in overly personal terms do not truly intend to reduce all of God's redemptive activity to their own personal sphere, the way we tell our stories matters. If the theory of narrative therapy is correct, the vocabulary of our stories can either open up our stories to new possibilities, or it can close them off into a single dead-end story. Expressing our experience of God's redemption in exclusively personal language limits our potential to grow in our appreciation for the marvelous height and breadth of God's capacious love.

By consciously including "my neighbor's story" in our complex of storytelling, we are reminded that God is not the small god of our imaginations, but the one whose love reaches far beyond what we can imagine and envelops in love the entirety of creation. Since God is the creator and sustainer of the universe, then every story is incomplete unless we place it within the larger story of God's radically inclusive salvation of the world.

A second reason why it is so important to include "my neighbor's story" into evangelism is to prevent our feeling we have to choose between evangelism and social justice. Most churches are committed to one or the other, but the truth is they can't exist without each other.

Concern for my neighbor, for his story, his world, his rights, his well-being — social justice — is what the news of God's radically inclusive love is all about. When Luke articulates the Great Commandment to love God and to love one's neighbor as oneself, he tells of a lawyer who challenges Jesus with the question, "Who is my neighbor?" In response, Jesus gives one of the most fascinating parables of the New Testament, the parable of the Good Samaritan. What is fascinating about this parable is that it demonstrates how love of God and neighbor overcomes one of the most intense dividing walls of prejudice known to Jesus' culture — the hatred between Jews and Samaritans. If we build our complex of stories on the three components of the Great Commandment, "my neighbor's story" can never be reduced to the periphery.

My Story: Receiving Grace, Responding with Gratitude

I believe that the third component of our three-storied experience presents the most challenges. Some folks have difficulties with this part because of their humility: they have trouble imagining that they really and truly are beloved children of God. It is one thing to say that God is loving, God is graceful, God claims us before we do anything deserving of judgment or grace, etc. It is another thing to appropriate these words to one's own life and say, "God loves me," "God is gracious to me," "God claims me as God's own beloved child." It is like the difference between saying "We all have to die some time" and saying, "What? I'm dying?"

For others, the difficulties with the third component of our three-storied experience lie elsewhere. Too often "my story" comes across as either too arrogant or too self-centered. The arrogance seems to arise from the "one-size-fits-all" mold in which "my story" seems to be the only template out there for an experience of God's grace. The self-centeredness seems to come from the problem that we have mentioned above, the implication that "it's all about me." Whether intentional or not, too many stories of one's salvation experience have turned people of faith off to the whole notion of telling "my story."

Once we establish that "God's story" is the story of God's initiative and that "my neighbor's story" is expressive of the expansiveness of God's love, we can begin to tell our own story without the fear of sounding arrogant or self-centered. Telling "my story" does not mean that my life is a perfect example of the gospel. It does not mean that my life is utter bliss and completely without pain, failure, or discouragement. And it does not mean that the good news of the gospel is all about me. In fact, one way that the Apostle Paul often told his story was by making frequent mention of his *weaknesses*, since, he argued, in our weakness Christ is made strong (2 Corinthians 12:9–10). The effective power of "my story" is precisely that it is *not* dependent on my performance or perfection. I am merely a witness to the grace of God in Christ, which has the power to redeem or heal me, even in my broken imperfection. Therefore, I can witness to the gospel by pointing to life-changing experiences, wonder-filled moments, as well as my sufferings or abysmal failures.

I find it helpful to think of "my story" as a two-part story. If the first emphasis of "God's story" is that God takes the initiative, then the human experience of "my story" should corroborate by emphasizing our receptivity of grace first. Therefore, the first part of "my story" is *receptive:* I have received God's grace when, through no merit of my own, God claimed me as God's own beloved child. The second part of "my story" is *responsive:* I live in response to the grace of God. To be sure, there are times when my response to God's grace is nothing to be proud of. There are times when I have doubted that I am God's beloved child — for good or bad reasons. There are times when I have been so wrapped up in my own life that I have failed to see my neighbors as God's beloved children. And, there are times when I have enjoyed the grace to live in what John Calvin once described as "a debt of gratitude." Like the Apostle Paul, "my story" is less about my perfections and accomplishments and more about my life as a recipient of grace. When we keep the initiative of "God's story" and the capaciousness of "my neighbor's story" in mind, we are free to share "my story" as a joyous response of gratitude to God's redemptive presence.

Conclusion: Evangelism Is Witnessing to the Joy and Justice of the Gospel

To live in a three-storied universe is to hold "God's story," "my neighbor's story," and "my story" together as three necessary components of our experience. I like to refer to this three-storied complex as "witnessing to the joy and justice of the gospel." It is, at its heart, giving our witness to the *gospel* — "God's story" of God's redemptive love made known in Christ. It is giving witness to the *justice* of the gospel, "my neighbor's story" of how God's redemptive love in Christ embraces the entirety of our world. And it is giving witness to the *joy* of the gospel, "my story" of how I have been embraced by God's redemptive presence and live responsively out of a debt of gratitude.

Kazuo Ishiguro's novels point us to the profound way that our personal story can be transformed by situating it within a larger story. As those who are called to share the joy and justice of the gospel, one of the best gifts we have to share with others is the larger story, "God's story," which gives us fresh and hopeful ways of encountering our stories anew.

Session Six

Witnessing to the
Joy and Justice of the Gospel

Introduction: Back to Sam

Eight years after my embarrassing evangelism encounter with Sam, I was in a children's toy store when I heard an unforgettable voice. It was Sam's wife, Debra, whose voice I had heard throughout high school as a disc jockey on a popular radio station. I followed the voice and found Debra, who introduced me to their children and told me that Sam was in the next aisle. When I found him he gave me his customary bear hug and asked me what in the world I was doing with myself. That was the beginning of my greatest lesson in how God is faithful even when our own actions fail miserably.

I explained to Sam that I was in the process of leaving the church tradition of my childhood. We talked about how difficult that decision was and all of the history that went into making it. I told him that I was looking to join a local Presbyterian church, with the intention of entering into the process of becoming a candidate for ordination.

Sam brightened up considerably and said, "Well, you need to come with me on Sunday morning! I'm an elder at Hilton Presbyterian Church and we would love to have you." I was stunned! I accepted Sam's invitation and joined his congregation for worship that Sunday, with Sam coming down from the choir loft to sit with me during the latter half of the service. Eventually I joined that church, and Sam had the role of introducing me to the church elders, telling them about our past together (but, to my relief, leaving the failed evangelism attempt out of the telling). In time it was also Sam who recommended me to be received by the elders as an "Inquirer" into ordination. Sam! The same Sam whom I tried to evangelize so awkwardly years before!

The good news of God's grace for anyone who aspires to evangelize came home to me quite clearly in my relationship with Sam. When we say that "God is faithful; we are not; God loves us anyway," we are not just summarizing the plot of stories in the Bible. We are not just naming the "three spiritual laws" that lead to a conversion experience. We are stating the essential starting and ending point of the entire activity of evangelism: God's redemptive presence is prior to our efforts, and while God will work in and through what we do, there are times that God will also work *despite* what we do. That bit of good news is both humbling and encouraging for those of us who are called to share the joy and justice of the gospel.

"God is faithful; we are not; God loves us anyway" means that our response to the call to evangelize is not measured by the quantity of conversions that we can count. It means that our best efforts *and* our most awkward, stuttered fiascos can equally be moments of grace for us or others. It means that, while God invites us to be a part of God's plan to save the world, that plan rests on God's redemptive presence in the world and not on our success.

One thing that I learned from my experience with Sam is that God's redemptive presence in Sam's life was far more effectual than my efforts. Despite my miserable attempt to convert him in his office, God was redemptively present in his life. Despite my own absence while away in college and seminary, God was present in Sam's life by way of a thousand other streams of grace. Sam's relationship with God did not hinge on my getting it right or saying just the right thing. With God's redemptive presence in the world, my own proficiency at evangelizing turned out to be a rather small piece of the picture.

For our last session, we will draw together the journey that we have traveled toward embracing anew our call to share the joy and justice of the gospel. Along this journey we have visited:

+ the critical role of genuine listening,
+ the core belief in God's redemptive activity in the world,
+ and the three-storied experience that we try to capture whenever we act as witnesses to God's grace.

We began with what I called "the quandary of evangelism" and have sought to express faithful ways to overcome that quandary. There remains one question, a significant question that goes to the very heart of the journey that we have shared together, which we will address as a way of bringing our journey to its conclusion. The question is whether or not *conversion* is a necessary part of evangelism. But before we answer that question, a review of where we have been is in order.

Revisiting the Quandary

A large part of the quandary of evangelism is that the *language* of evangelism has come to evoke too many negative images, especially for many people who have been on the receiving end of coercive evangelistic efforts.[18] The German philosopher of language Hans-Georg Gadamer argues that words have "an effective historical consciousness."[19] By that he means that words gather meaning through historical events, sometimes to the point that words indelibly signify ideas far away from their original meaning. The word "inquisition," for example, has its root in the word "inquiry." As such, it is a rather benign word. However, for those of us who live on this side of the historical event called "The Inquisition," the term "inquisition" has picked up a rather sinister connotation that follows it everywhere.

Perhaps the word "evangelism" is indelibly tainted with overtones of coercion in the same way that the word "inquisition" now evokes images of violence. That would be such a shame for a word that should connote a lovely activity of sharing good news.

Our focus throughout this text has been on the *activity* of evangelism. We have seen that the quandary of evangelism arises when acting on the Great Commission to evangelize seems to be in tension with obeying the Great Commandment to love. As a result, people of faith and good will often find themselves with the unhappy quandary of either doing something that feels intrusive and obnoxious, or not sharing the gospel with their neighbor. The quandary is both ironic and tragic.

Summary of Our Journey

Throughout this book, we have explored a way of sharing the joy and justice of the gospel that gets us beyond the quandary of evangelism. With attention to both principles and practices, we have explored a way of being faithful to the Great Commission to make disciples without running roughshod over the Great Commandment to love our neighbors. Below is a summary of the principles and practices that we have discussed and the advantages that they bring toward overcoming the quandary of evangelism.

When we begin with the principle that God is redemptively present in the world...

* Human sinfulness is not the beginning point of our stories;
* being claimed as God's beloved child is the beginning of our stories.
* The threat of hell is not the motivation for salvation;
* living in joyful response to God's grace is our motivation for salvation.
* The success of the evangelist is not the linchpin for redemption;
* the grace of God that overcomes our failures is what makes evangelism effective.

When we practice genuine listening...

- We avoid monologues disguised as conversations;
- we see dialogue as a way of discovering God's redemptive presence in the world.
- We avoid miscommunications, like "Tata Jesus is Bängala!";
- we discover expansive ways of expressing God's love.
- We avoid treating the other's story as devoid of God's grace;
- we affirm God's redemptive presence in the other person's life.

When we share the gospel by telling our three-storied experience...

- We find meaningful ways of connecting *God's story* with *my story.*
- We find meaningful ways of connecting *God's story* with *my neighbor's story.*
- We find meaningful ways of affirming God's redemptive presence in the world.

The kinds of principles, activities, and practices that we have explored in this book move us constructively beyond the quandary of evangelism and offer ways of sharing the joy and justice of the gospel without violating the call to love one's neighbor. Even if our stories are full of passion and conviction, even if it is our fondest hope that others would accept the good news of God's love for their own lives, when we rely on God's redemptive presence in the world and practice genuine listening, then we can tell our stories in ways that are invitational but not argumentative.

A Remaining Question: Must Evangelism Include Conversion?

There is one significant question remaining that we must address in order to move past the quandary of evangelism with confidence. According to many definitions of evangelism, the kinds of activities that we have explored in this book may be uplifting and encouraging but do not truly constitute evangelism unless they include *conversion* as their ultimate goal. The question is "If there is no conversion, is it truly evangelism?" This pivotal question goes to the heart of whether, without conversion as its goal, the activities of listening for God's redemptive presence in the world and telling one's story are evangelism proper or simply worthy activities.

Eddie Fox and George Morris have argued that it is symptomatic of our success-driven culture that sharing one's faith is often confused with the goal of converting others to one's faith. Fox and Morris conclude that "this is a common mistake. We forget that it is God who converts."[20]

I agree with Fox's and Morris's conclusion, particularly their insight that sharing the gospel is our calling while conversion is God's work. However, I also feel that the issue of associating evangelism with conversion is more than just an outgrowth of our modern understanding of success. Those who quantify successful evangelism by pointing to numbers of converts — whether it is the "numbers of souls being saved" or church membership statistics as an indication of success or failure — often do so as a way of being faithful to the scriptures. In the book of Acts, where the story of the early church gives us most of our scriptural understanding of evangelism, there are numbers being touted everywhere! On the Day of Pentecost, three thousand people were baptized (2:41). After the lame man is healed at the Beautiful Gate, five thousand people heard Peter's sermon and believed (4:4). Elsewhere it says, "Day by day the Lord added to their number those who were being saved" (2:47). One could easily argue that quantifying faithful evangelism began with Luke, the author of Acts, not with the modern understanding of success.

As I see it, the most troubling aspect of confusing evangelism with conversion is not the success-driven, number-crunching tendencies of our culture. The most significant issue is that the dynamics of power that have changed dramatically from the time of the early church to today. And without sensitivity to that significant change, evangelism will lead to coercive attempts at conversion. Therefore, while we rightly get our bearings regarding evangelism from the witness of the scriptures, we must also add to our reading of the scriptures our experience of historical consciousness in order to be faithful to the gospel for our context today. For our last study of scripture, we will look at a bold witness from the book of Acts and then consider how the dynamics of power have shifted between then and now in order to be faithful to sharing the gospel today.

A Study of Scripture, with History in Mind

One of the greatest accounts of evangelism in the early church is found in the twenty-sixth chapter of the book of Acts. Paul, an evangelist, gives a very bold, personal testimony of his own conversion experience to a man named Agrippa. At one point, Agrippa asks Paul, "Are you so quickly persuading me to become a Christian?" Paul answers, "Whether quickly or not, I pray to God that not only you but all who are listening to me today might become such as I am. . . . "

On the face of it, this story could be construed as the worst kind of presumptuous evangelism imaginable. Paul tells his story and arrogantly expects to convert everyone who hears it to become as he is. However, I have not told this story in its entirety. In this story, Paul is a prisoner, standing on trial for his Christian preaching. Agrippa is a regional king who represents something like an appellate court. In fact, Paul's answer to King Agrippa's question is actually, "I pray to God that not only you but all who are listening to me today might become such as I am — *except for these chains.*"

The key to this story is that Paul is completely powerless, relying entirely on the power of his testimony to be persuasive. It would be a totally different story if the dynamics of power were switched, with Paul in the position of authority and Agrippa in chains. Then, Paul's words would have a totally different demeanor to them and Paul's intent to "convert" would be more of an act of coercion. If

"King Paul" had tried to persuade "Agrippa the prisoner" to convert to following Jesus Christ, this would be a different story entirely.

When we encounter this story with history in mind, we must admit that something significant happened in history when Christianity went from being a minority religion of courageous faith to being a major religious institution. Simply put, the dynamics of power did switch. The church no longer speaks out of a position of powerlessness; therefore the same words, the same attempts to persuade — originally spoken from a position of powerlessness — are now impacted by an "effective historical consciousness," much like the words "inquisition" and "evangelism."

At least in Western societies, the dynamics of power have changed dramatically since Paul stood enchained before King Agrippa. In his book *A Violent Evangelism*, Luis Rivera gives many mind-boggling accounts of how the powerful Christian church inflicted terrible violence in the name of the gospel during the early missionary movement, even to the point of justifying the murder of those who refused to accept Jesus Christ.[21] Sharing the joy and justice of the gospel today means being sensitive to living on this side of such a history of violence in the name of the gospel. While such overt violence is certainly uncommon today, the Christian church continues to assume certain types of power that can transform courageous attempts to persuade, such as Paul in chains before King Agrippa, to coercive attempts to convert, such as King Paul and the prisoner Agrippa.

One might argue that the powerlessness of the early church was simply a historical phenomenon of the church's infancy, with little implications as to how evangelism should be practiced today. However, the Apostle Paul did not see the early church's lack of coercive power as a historical accident. For Paul, the church's weakness was the very manner in which God is redemptively present in the world:

> Consider your own call, brothers and sisters: not many of you were wise by human standards, not many were powerful,

not many were of noble birth. But God chose what is foolish in the world to shame the wise; God chose what is weak in the world to shame the strong; God chose what is low and despised in the world, things that are not, to reduce to nothing things that are, so that no one might boast in the presence of God (1 Corinthians 1:26–29).

The changes in the dynamics of power from Paul's enslaved witness before King Agrippa to today carry important implications for evangelism. If God chooses the weak and despised in the world to demonstrate God's power, then the church will not have the power of persuasion unless we rediscover what it means to find God's power within our own weakness. It is only when followers of Jesus Christ give up our presumption of power and let go of manipulation, coercion, and other ways in which evangelism has been practiced throughout history that we can truly recapture the kind of persuasive witness that the Apostle Paul demonstrates before King Agrippa. Therefore, it is my contention that, in our day, attempts to convert others must be replaced by a deliberate attempt to relinquish the kind of power that the Christian church has adopted through history.

For that reason, this book and our discussions have not been about how to persuade others, how to outwit people's arguments, how to present the specter of punishment and eternal damnation to the lost, or how to deconstruct other people's belief systems. *Rather, we have focused on genuine listening as a way of relinquishing power and relying on the redemptive presence of God to change hearts and minds.* Our call is to be a witness to the joy and justice of the gospel wherever we find it, in our own lives as well as in the lives of others.

Conclusion

I wish I had understood God's redemptive presence in the world better when, in my zeal to follow the Great Commission, I attempted to evangelize Sam. It was certainly my intention to "convert" him by convincing him that he was lost and stood con-demned without accepting the gospel as I understood it. If I had had stronger faith in God's redemptive presence in Sam's life, I might have spent time genuinely listening to Sam's story, hearing what troubles him, what delights him, what makes him passionate or despairing. If I had learned to leave conversion up to God, I might have discovered that God was already redemptively present in Sam's life in ways that I could not have imagined. With less reliance on my own powers of persuasion, I might have learned that what I perceived as unbelief in Sam was a dissatisfaction with the church's practices — the very practices I was following in try-ing to evangelize him! And if I had simply shared my story with Sam, I might have discovered that he was quite open to hearing what was meaningful to me, but not my attempt to convert him. As I look back on that day in Sam's office, I feel that I was doing everything I had been trained to do to follow the Great Commis-sion to evangelize Sam — but that I was stomping all over the Great Commandment to love Sam in the process.

What I discovered eight years after my disastrous attempt to evangelize Sam was that God's redemptive presence in the world is strangely greater than we can imagine. Quite apart from my powers of persuasion, Sam found a worshiping community where his faith could flourish. In an ironic twist of God's grace, it was Sam who took on the role of introducing me into that community and into my journey of ordination as a pastor.

That mysterious, forgiving, and occasionally ironic experience of God's grace is the only basis for witnessing to the joy and justice of the gospel without being arrogant or intrusive. Because of God's grace, there is a way of following the Great Commission without violating the Great Commandment. It is by God's grace that we can share the joy and justice of the gospel by genuinely listening for God's redemptive presence in our world. My hope is that you, too, can experience the mind-boggling grace of God as you find mean-ingful ways of sharing your story, genuinely listening to others, and discovering anew how God is redemptively present in our world.

DISCUSSION
GUIDES

DISCUSSION GUIDE
TO SESSION ONE:
Diagnosing the Quandary of Evangelism

Class Objective

The purpose of this first session is to deconstruct or take apart the model of evangelism that has given a bad name to what should be a lovely and loving activity. Instead of loveliness, many people perceive evangelism as an obnoxious activity that is more defined by arrogance than agape. In this session we will explore what it is about evangelism that makes it so off-putting for people of faith as well as for those who are outside of the Christian faith.

After this session our conversation will turn toward reconstructing evangelism as a way of sharing the joy and justice of the gospel.

Materials Needed

- Newsprint and colored markers (black, red, blue, and green – or substitute your own)
- Pen and paper for each participant
- Hymnals or songbooks from your church
- Bibles

Opening Introductions

Within every denominational group there are those who like the current models of evangelism and those who for some reason dislike them. Therefore, in your group discussion that follows, it is possible that group members will have difficult and awkward experiences to share. The key to a fruitful discussion is to create an atmosphere where everyone feels free to openly express to each other either their attachment to or their resentment of current models of evangelism. To develop that openness, begin the conversation by having the group members introduce themselves and answer the following questions.

+ *What brings you into a group conversation on evangelism? What does that tell us about you?*

+ The Introduction to this book describes a "quandary of evangelism" this way: "Something that should be a joyous, natural activity for those who follow Christ appears to be a forced, coercive activity unfitting for those who follow Christ." *In what ways do you agree with this argument regarding the quandary of evangelism?*

Sharing Experiences:
Exploring Our Own "Evangelism Encounters"

After reading the story of my evangelism encounter with Sam, each class member is invited to think of an evangelism encounter from her own experience and to be prepared to share it with the group. For this activity, make sure that each person has a pen and paper. As one person shares the story of an evangelism encounter, ask the others to listen for and record the *intentions* that they imagine the evangelizing person brought to the encounter and the *feelings* that they imagine the evangelized person experienced.

After the group members have shared their stories, compile a master list of "intentions" on one sheet and a list of "feelings" on another sheet of newsprint. (We will return to these lists in the second session, so make sure to keep them for later use.) Now, as a group, identify the following:

+ Mark the intentions or feelings that are **common** to several encounters with red underlines.

+ Mark the **negative** intentions or feelings with **blue** underlines.

+ Mark the **positive** intentions or feelings with **green** underlines.

Now, with this visual identification of the intentions and feelings involved in evangelism encounters, we are ready to explore Bishop Spong's remarks.

Hashing It Out:
Bishop Spong's Criticisms of Evangelism

Ask the group turn to the quote by Bishop Spong, found on page 21, and study it together by answering the following questions:

◆ What are the "manifestations of hostility" to which Spong is referring?

◆ Which of the "intentions" that we have identified support Spong's claim that evangelistic practices show "manifestations of hostility"?

◆ Which of the "feelings" that we have identified support Spong's claim that evangelistic practices show "manifestations of hostility"?

◆ Spong says that the hostility and attempts to convert Jews grow out of a theological assumption "that one tradition possesses the sole route to God." Was this true of our own stories that we have shared?

◆ Spong's response to problems with evangelism is to reject evangelism as an activity, calling it "unworthy of the Christ figure." What other possible responses to problems with evangelism can you imagine?

At this point, your discussion group may have come to conclusions ranging anywhere from "Spong is wrong" to "He's right; let's go home." Whether we agree with Spong's response of rejecting evangelism or envision the possibility of redeeming evangelism, we will take Spong's criticisms seriously.

A Study of Scripture: The Roman Road to Salvation

On page 24 of this text you will find a listing of the four scripture verses that comprise the "Roman Road to Salvation." Each participant has been invited to consider some questions about the "Roman Road" in preparation for this discussion. I offered some answers to these questions, but the more important responses will arise from the group members themselves.

◆ Out of all of the contents of Paul's letter to Rome, why do you imagine these texts are specifically selected for evangelism?

◆ Is it the typical New Testament model of evangelism to begin with human sinfulness and condemnation? What other texts or models come to mind?

◆ What kind of claim is one making about God and humanity if the first step of the Roman Road begins by declaring the fallen and accursed state of humanity?

◆ What other claims about God and humanity come to your mind as a better "first step" to share with others?

Faithful Reflections:
Listening to Our Traditions

Our critique of the Roman Road may lead us to construct a more promising way of expressing the good news of the gospel. On page 23, each participant was invited to select a favorite song and to think about what that song says regarding God's stance toward humanity and humanity's standing before God. For this discussion, hymnals or songbooks from the group's worship services should be available so that each person can follow along the text of the songs if possible. (This exercise may work best in smaller groups of three or four.)

Ask each person to tell the others which hymn or song she selected and why. As the group considers the lyrics of each song, ask each person to offer a one-word description about God that emerges from their favorite songs, and write these down. For example, a person who selects the song, "O Sacred Head, Now Wounded," might say that God is "merciful" to come to us through such suffering. Or a person who selects "God of the Sparrow" might describe God as "awesome." (For this exercise it will be helpful to compile words expressed about God, Jesus, and the Holy Spirit together as one.)

Save these one-word descriptions for the next class session.

Closing Prayer

As a way of closing this first gathering, invite the group to voice a prayer based on the insights that you have shared during the session. For this prayer, have the lists of one-word descriptions of God and the lists of feelings and intentions visible for the entire group.

- Going around the circle, invite each person to look at the list of one-word descriptions of God and, using one of the words on the list, offer a prayer beginning with the words, **"We thank you for . . .** [the awesome beauty of creation.]**"**

- Going around the circle a second time, invite each person to look at the list of intentions and feelings at play in our previous evangelism encounters and to offer a prayer beginning with the words, **"Forgive us when we . . .** [fail to show mercy to others].**"**

- Let the session leader close the prayer with these words:

    **Grant us the grace to share your good news
    in ways that are worthy of followers of Christ. Amen.**

DISCUSSION GUIDE TO SESSION TWO: The Great Commission and the Initiative of Evangelism

Class Objective

The goal of this class is to move from a deconstructive critique of previous models of evangelism toward reconstructing a positive model of evangelism.

Materials Needed

- Newsprint and markers
- A trash can (or recycling bin)
- The master lists of "intentions" and "feelings" from the first session
- The list of "one-word descriptions" of God from the first session

Review and Renew

In the first session, the group identified *intentions* and *feelings* at work in our shared stories of evangelism encounters. By *intentions* we mean the motives and hopes of the person who is evangelizing. By *feelings* we mean the reactions of the person being evangelized.

Some of the intentions and feelings that were identified in the first meeting might be appropriate for evangelism, but many of them will not. In this exercise, we will begin with the previous list in order to create new lists of intentions and feelings that are more appropriate to sharing the good news of the gospel.

- Begin by having the *intentions* and *feelings* lists from the first session on display along with blank sheets of newsprint with the same headings for new lists.
- From the master list of *intentions,* invite the group to identify *appropriate* intentions for evangelism and carry them over to the new

86

list. Then imagine what intentions would be ideal for evangelism and add them to the new list.

◆ Second, do the same with the master list of *feelings:* identify *appropriate* feelings to carry to the new list and imagine the feelings that ideally would be evoked.

Now, with the new lists, we have the beginnings of a direction for evangelism that takes us beyond the problems that we have identified in our first session.

Ritual of Moving On

This exercise is an invitation for the group to put their negative experiences of evangelism encounters firmly behind them. The symbol is a trash can. It is important to recognize how destructive previous models of evangelism have been for many people. At the same time, for those who have had *positive* evangelism encounters along the way, it may be important to point out that we have already salvaged the appropriate intentions and feelings from the first discussion prior to this exercise.

◆ Invite the group, one by one, to tear off a portion of the list from the first discussion and to dispose of it with the words, "The gospel is the *good news* of God's love" (or with words of their own choosing).

◆ When the former lists are completely gone, turn the group's attention to the list of one-word descriptions of God that the group compiled in the first session from songs in the hymn book. Using those one-word descriptions to fill in the blank, invite the group to voice prayers with the words, "[*Awesome*] God, show us a way of sharing the good news of your love."

◆ Remove the trash can or recycle bin from the room as a final sign of moving past the forms of evangelism that are unworthy of God's love.

Rereading the Great Commission

Invite the group to turn to the *shaded box version* of the Great Commission found on page 32 in your book. I have argued that this commission is not primarily a "marching order" for the church but a promise of Christ's presence and work in the world. Invite the participants to evaluate this argument through the following questions:

+ What do you think is the primary focal point of Matthew's Great Commission?

+ Does reading Luke's version of the Great Commission (Acts 1:8) change the way that you read Matthew's version of it (Matthew 28:19–20)?

+ I argue that Christ's presence is primarily important in the Great Commission. If that is correct, what implications does that have for our call to share the good news of God's love?

Witnessing to God's Redemptive Presence in the World

Turn the group's attention to the statement from George Stroup, found on page 35 in your book. I use this quote to argue that our calling from the Great Commission is primarily to be *witnesses* by following Christ's "redemptive presence" in the world. For some, this may be far too passive an approach to evangelism. Therefore, I invited readers to think of some metaphors, imagery, or parables in the New Testament that emphasize Christ's initiative and our "following," as opposed to our initiative in Christ's absence. Invite the class to share those thoughts now.

Closing Prayer

It is a different approach to evangelism to consider oneself as a follower or a witness to what Christ is doing rather than as the one taking initiative. For some, it means a prayer for humility is in order;

for others, even being a witness requires a prayer for more boldness. Invite the group to join in the following closing prayer:

> **Living, present, active God:**
> **Grant us the humility to marvel at your presence**
> **and the boldness to share your good news as witnesses.**
> **Amen.**

DISCUSSION GUIDE
TO SESSION THREE:
Evangelism as Conversation:
Listening

Class Objective

The purpose of this class is to identify the principles for a practice of evangelism in a world where God is always already redemptively present.

Materials Needed

* Bibles
* Side-by-side charts of the "I-You Components" on page 41 and the "Godly Presumptions" from page 46.

The Story of John and "Evangelism"

I have represented the story of my relationship with John as an evangelism story. However, there was no prayer of repentance, "no conversion experience," and no profession of Jesus Christ as Lord and Savior. Discuss the story beginning with the following questions:

* Is this an "evangelism" story? Why or why not?
* Would John's life be better if there had been a prayer of repentance or a dramatic "conversion experience" in this story?
* In what ways could we say that God was "already redemptively present" in John's life?
* In what ways could we say that John was "estranged" from God?
* What does John's story suggest for the role of "listening" in evangelism?
* Again: Is this an "evangelism" story or not?

Building Blocks for Doing Evangelism

On pages 40–41 I provide two principles on which to build a theology of evangelism. The first is, "Originally and primarily, each one belongs to God." The second is, "The redemptive presence and work of Christ goes before us." We will revisit these two principles throughout the remaining sessions. For now, it is important to clarify together what these two principles mean to the group members. We will do so by looking at the story of the Prodigal Son in Luke 15:11–32.

+ I have identified the turning point of this popular parable as that moment when the Prodigal Son "came to himself" (v. 17). In what way does the Prodigal Son represent the first principle of theology, "Originally and primarily, each one belongs to God"

+ The father tells the older brother that the younger son "was dead and has come to life; he was lost and is now found" (v. 32). How does this story shape the way that we might think of what it means to be "lost"?

+ Paul Tillich uses the word "estrangement" to describe the experience of being lost. How does the word "estrangement" affect our understanding of this parable?

+ This is the parable of a son, who originally and primarily belongs in his father's house, but has strayed far away. What kind of guidance does this parable offer for the practice of evangelism?

"I-You Components" versus "Godly Presumptions": Retelling Our Stories

For this exercise, post a listing of what I call the "I-You Components" on page 41 next to a listing of the "Godly Presumptions" on page 46. Recall that in the first session participants were invited to share their stories of evangelism encounters. Those encounters are often painful because the relational dynamics of the "I-You Components" are at work.

- Invite those whose evangelism encounters were painful to reimagine their stories with the "Godly Presumptions" at work as the terms of the conversation. How might that conversation have gone differently?

- Can the participants think of relationships that they have had where the "Godly Presumptions" have been at work? (Examples might include parent-child relationships, friendships, missionary partnerships, etc.) Have the participants ever considered such relationships as "evangelism" before? If not, why not?

Closing Prayer

For a closing prayer, invite group members to consider a person in their lives who seems to be living an "estranged" life. With those persons' faces in mind, ask the group to offer prayers on behalf of those who are estranged and ask God to grant the wisdom so that we might be faithful companions in bringing them to that moment when they "come to themselves."

DISCUSSION GUIDE TO SESSION FOUR:
Listening and Telling

Class Objective

The goal of this class is to practice genuine listening and consider why it is so important to telling the good news in evangelism.

Materials Needed

+ Bibles

+ Space for play acting

Listening to a Monologue

A number of group games bring to light the difficulties of communication, especially when the communication is a one-sided monologue. The game that is sometimes called "Telephone" (perhaps more aptly named "Gossip") demonstrates how messages get contorted as they are passed from mouth to ear around the circle. Games like "Charades" demonstrate how word-dependent we are, as well as how differing sets of expectations cause us to see the same gesture in multiple ways. The following game is a combination of Charades and Telephone, because it involves pantomiming a story from person to person. So find a little space, don't be shy, and have fun together learning how vital it is for good communication to be able both to listen and to tell.

The key to a good story for this exercise is that it is simple, with some interesting and unexpected elements to it. Here is a beginning story:

I was at the zoo on a hot day eating an ice cream cone when an elephant sprayed me with water. It felt good, but I threw the ice cream cone away.

1. Begin with a designated storyteller and a "listener." (Others are out of the room for the moment.)

2. The storyteller pantomimes the story above to the listener, one time only. (Unlike Charades, the listener just watches, without interacting.)

3. The listener then becomes storyteller #2 as another person is brought into the room to listen. (The original storyteller now gets to sit and watch, observing how the story changes each time it is told.)

4. Storyteller #2 pantomimes the story and then sits down as another person is brought in and the listener becomes storyteller #3 to the next person.

5. The story gets retold until all of the participants are in the room. The last person to "listen" to the story then verbally tells the story to the whole group.

The group can repeat this exercise, with the first person deciding the story to act out. When you are done, here are questions for reflection:

♦ What happened to the story from its origin to its final form?

♦ What were the hard parts to act out?

♦ What parts were hard to understand as the "listener"?

♦ If the listener had been able to ask questions or request that a part of the story to be repeated, how might the pantomiming have been different? What does this tell you about the advantages and function of a dialogue over a monologue in communicating?

♦ Which member of the group deserves an Oscar award for "Best Dramatic Performance with a Thin Plot"?

Tata Jesus Is Bängala!

Session 4 (page 47) begins with a reference to Barbara Kingsolver's book *The Poisonwood Bible*, where a missionary miscommunicates because he is unwilling to listen and learn from the people whom he is evangelizing. When the missionary says "Tata Jesus is Bängala!"

his message is completely distorted. Remind the group of this opening story and invite them to share with the group: *Tell of a "Tata
Jesus is Bängala!" experience when you tried to communicate one
thing, but actually miscommunicated because of a failure to know
your audience.*

Now we will turn to an experience where someone took the
time to listen to his audience's story and was therefore able to
communicate the gospel effectively.

Paul in Athens

Invite the group to look up the story of Paul's experience in Acts
17:16–34. From this story, I have drawn the following points, found
on pages 51–53:

1. Paul begins by noting that the Athenians are extremely religious.

2. One altar in particular provides Paul with an opportunity to share
   the gospel.

3. Paul presents a bold and faithful message of God's grace.

4. Paul's message of God's grace *includes* the Athenians' own
   expressions of piety.

5. Paul finds greater expression of his own faith as a result of
   genuine listening.

Looking especially at points 4 and 5, study this text by using the
following questions:

♦ In what way does Paul's message of God's grace include the
   Athenians' own expressions of piety?

♦ In what way does Paul find greater expression for his own faith as
   a result of genuine listening?

♦ Who are some people in your life with whom you might share
   the gospel, but whose own story you need to hear first? (Answers might range from a Muslim colleague to a neighbor who
   has nothing but bitter things to say about faith.)

Breaking the Ice

One of the more awkward moments of evangelism — especially if one is following the "I-You Components" — is the moment of "breaking the ice" by bringing up the topic of faith. It is not for nothing that many people say religion is one of the forbidden topics at the dinner table! Perhaps the whole awkwardness could be avoided if we think of "breaking the ice" as a moment — not of asking someone "are you saved?" but of inviting someone to tell his or her own faith story or journey. It may still be awkward, but much less so than immediately imposing one's own agenda and language on another.

In this exercise, encourage participants to break up into groups of two and to practice "breaking the ice." Ask them to converse with each other and find natural ways of inviting the other to tell her story, specifically listening for stories of faith, passion, survival, or even of deep anger. The point is not to give a timeline of church membership, but to speak about that which is truly meaningful for one's life.

Closing and Prayer

Invite the group to regather, and debrief the previous exercise with these questions:

+ What was the most awkward part about inviting another person to share her story?
+ What was the most awkward part about being asked to share your story?
+ What were some nice surprises you discovered along the way?
+ How would this "breaking the ice" experience be different outside of this study group's experience?

Invite the members of the group to offer a tailor-made prayer for the person whose story they have just heard. Encourage them to think of things for which to give thanks, as well as challenges to express concern. Due to the very personal nature of some of the stories that have been shared, ask the participants to accept this prayer for what it is — a public prayer in front of the storyteller —

recognizing that a private prayer might be much more candid and less self-conscious.

Then let the leader end the prayer with these words:

> **Gracious God:**
> **as you have made yourself known to us**
> **through the story of Jesus Christ,**
> **help us to find ways to learn and celebrate**
> **your continually unfolding story**
> **in the lives of the people we meet. Amen.**

DISCUSSION GUIDE TO SESSION FIVE: Telling Stories Faithfully

Class Objective

The goal of this session is to find faithful, authentic ways to tell our stories, using the three-storied approach of God's story, my neighbor's story, and my story.

Materials Needed

◆ Bibles

◆ Newsprint and colored markers (black, red, blue, and green — or substitute your own)

◆ Newspapers from the previous week (sections with local, national, or international news are best, not sports, comics, or entertainment)

◆ Paper and pens for everyone

Dynamic Storytelling

I describe how, in narrative therapy, the therapist invites a client to tell her story and then offers a larger story — a larger set of images and vocabulary — so that the client can tell her story again, but differently. For this opening exercise, discuss the contribution that evangelism can receive from narrative therapy through mapping the following example on newsprint.

Example: A man loses his mobility through a car accident and goes through a very natural period of intense emotions. During this time, he tells his story using words like "handicap" and "cripple," with an overtone of disgust. If his story were to remain unchanged over a long period, it would be a "dead-end" story in the sense that he has resigned himself to being a "cripple."

Write in blue on the center of the newsprint: "Because of an accident, I am a cripple." (Your group may have objections to this choice of language. Those objections are well-founded, but this language is reflective of a dead end story and will be transformed through this exercise.)

Group question: After hearing this man's story and affirming it, what are some *words* that a narrative companion can offer for this man to envision his disability differently?

Using a red marker, write the words that the group offers as a larger concentric circle on the newsprint, surrounding the original story. Possibilities include: differently abled, different, life-change, opportunity, and so on.

Group question: However justified it might be, the *image* that comes to mind in the original story is that of a "bitter victim." Without denying the validity behind the bitterness or the sense of victimization, what are some other images that are available as a way of telling this story?

Using a green marker, write the brief descriptions of alternative images that the group offers on the newsprint, intermingled with the red vocabulary. Possibilities are: courageous survivor, disability advocate, fiercely independent, and so on.

Group question: With full view of the blue original story, red potential vocabulary, and green potential images, what are three authentic, but different possibilities for retelling this man's story? Remind the group that the original story is also authentic. Our purpose is not to deny that story, but to offer alternative ways of telling it.

Present the following summary to the group: *Through this exercise we can begin to see the theory behind narrative therapy. Of course, a therapeutic situation will require a lot more work than we have experienced, but this exercise prepares us for our next step of telling our three-storied experience.*

Encountering Our Three-Storied Experience

I have described a three-storied approach to our experience, calling it "God's story, my neighbor's story, and my story." We will look at each of these story components separately and then put them together as we begin to tell of our own three-storied experiences. For this exercise each participant should have paper and a pen. On the paper each person will write three brief descriptions — of God's story, my neighbor's story, and my story.

God's Story

On page 63 I have identified several biblical stories to describe "God's story" as having a simple three-part plot: God is faithful; we are not; God loves us anyway. Invite the participants to write down a brief description of "God's story" in whatever way means the most to them. This could take the form of a story from the scriptures, a composite of several biblical stories, or just a general description of God's way with us.

One example of a *Bible story* could be the story of the Prodigal Son from Luke 15.

An example of a *composite story* might be the story of Jesus and Simon Peter. After Peter boldly declares that he would never betray Jesus, Jesus predicts that Peter will deny him three times before the rooster crows. While Jesus is on trial, Peter does deny knowing Jesus, three different times. After the resurrection, Jesus asks Peter, also three times, "Peter do you love me?" By giving Peter three opportunities to express his love, Jesus helps Peter to overcome one of the most despairing failures of his life.

An example of a *general description of God's way with us* might be the lyrics from a particularly meaningful hymn, like "Amazing Grace."

My Neighbor's Story

I argue that "my neighbor's story" is the component in the three-storied experience that is left out of too many accounts of "personal salvation" (page 64). In addition, I argue that making "my neighbor's story" a necessary component of our three-storied experience helps to overcome the unwarranted division between evangelism and social justice.

For this exercise, distribute the newspapers from the previous week and invite each person to find an interesting "neighbor's" story. ("Neighbor" can be interpreted in a local or distant sense.) Ask the participants to consider this question as they select an article: *How does this "neighbor's story" relate to the way that I have described "God's story"?*

> One example might be a story of a conflict in another country that has raged between ethnic groups for many years. The story may point to the extreme difficulties of reconciliation, with so many years of resentment and distrust between the ethnic groups. If my telling of "God's story" had been the story of Jesus and Peter, I might relate the deep-seated resentment and distrust to the repetition of Jesus' question to Peter, "Do you love me?" Sometimes the path to reconciliation is a long journey that has to work its way down below superficial reparations and get to a deeper level of forgiveness. It might even be exasperating, as Jesus' questions were to Peter.

Now, ask each person to write down "my neighbor's story" as the second component of their three-storied experience.

My Story

Finally it is time to write "my story." I identify two types of difficulties with telling "my story." The first is the problem of humility and doubt: It is one thing to say that God loves everyone, another to look at one's life and say confidently "God loves me." The other problem is that too many stories of faith seem either too arrogant or too self-centered. Discuss with the group ways of telling one's story apart from arrogance or self-centeredness through answering the following questions:

+ What are three qualities of my personality or abilities that I have that I can describe as "gifts from God"?

+ What are two qualities of my personality about which I can only say "God loves me despite this"?

+ How can I tell my own faith story in a way that preserves God's initiative found in "God's story."

+ When I look at "my neighbor's story," how does it affect the way that I respond to God's grace?

With attention to God's initiative found in "God's story" and our world of neighbors found in "my neighbor's story," invite the group to write down a brief description of "my story" as the third and final component of their three-storied experience.

Closing Prayer

The point of putting our story on paper is to find faithful and authentic ways to share the joy and justice of the gospel. Invite the participants to conclude this activity with the following prayer:

> **Gracious, loving God:**
> **May our stories do justice**
> **to your grace and love.**
> **World-embracing God:**
> **May our stories be faithful**
> **to your capacious and expansive care**
> **for all the earth. Amen.**

DISCUSSION GUIDE TO SESSION SIX:
Witnessing to the Joy and Justice of the Gospel

Class Objective

The goal of this class is to consider how our study has taken us beyond the quandary of evangelism and to make a covenant for evangelism together.

Materials Needed

+ Bibles
+ A large common copy of the covenant found on page 107

Revisiting the Quandary of Evangelism

Our study began by naming a quandary of evangelism, namely, that many attempts to follow the Great Commission seem to violate the Great Commandment. In the first discussion, participants were invited to share their own stories of "evangelism encounters." Begin this discussion by inviting participants to recall those stories and to revisit them in light of the following questions:

+ What does the conclusion to the story of Sam say to you about God's redemptive presence and the activity of evangelism?
+ How does the conclusion to the story of Sam offer new meaning to your own evangelism encounter?
+ What does the conclusion to the story of Sam suggest for how you will practice evangelism?

Conversion and the Dynamics of Power

In the first discussion, we focused on Bishop John Shelby Spong's argument that it is time to abandon evangelism as an activity that is unworthy of the Christ figure. I have argued for a model of evangelism that invites genuine listening and relinquishes conversion as a goal by relying on God's redemptive presence in the world. Now ask the class to look back at Spong's argument (page 21) and discuss the following questions:

* How does the inclusion of "genuine listening" in session 3 address Spong's criticisms of evangelism?

* How does the argument to relinquish conversion as a goal of evangelism in session 6 address Spong's criticisms of evangelism?

* How has the description of evangelism in this book offered you a way of taking Spong's criticisms seriously while still embracing the activity of evangelism?

A Study of Scripture

The point of evangelism is not just to think correctly about it, but to practice it while thinking correctly about it. Therefore, we will end this time together by making a covenant for evangelism. Prior to that activity, invite the group to turn to the twenty-fourth chapter of Joshua. This is the story of how the people of Israel, after conquering the Promised Land, gathered in a town called Shechem to renew their covenant with God. Several features of this story make it an appropriate focus for our last session for this class. Begin by pointing out the following features:

* Shechem is a town that was never conquered, so the people gathered there that day represent *many different experiences of faith.*

* Joshua begins this covenant ceremony by *telling the story* of how God called and rescued them.

* Joshua invites the people to *respond* to the grace that they have *received* by renewing their covenant with God.

* Joshua *invites* those who have previously served other gods to join with them in this covenant.

Now read this summary to the group and invite them to follow along in their Bibles:

This story includes many of the features of evangelism that our book has presented. But very quickly this story takes a strange twist. In verse 18, the people agree to renew their covenant with God as Joshua has invited them saying, "We also will serve the Lord, for he is our God." Suddenly, Joshua "pushes back" at their attempt to renew their covenant, by saying, "You cannot serve the Lord" (v. 19). Joshua refuses to allow the people to step into this covenant lightly, so he resists their profession of loyalty to God.

The people will not be denied. They press even harder in verse 21 arguing, "No, we will serve the Lord!" Finally, Joshua relents and makes a covenant with them, writing down what had happened, setting up a memorial for the occasion, and sending them off.

Explore the implications that this story has for making covenants with the following questions:

- Why do you think Joshua says "You cannot serve the Lord" in v. 19?
- What does Joshua's reaction in v. 19 suggest about the act of making a covenant?
- What does the people's insistence (vv. 21 and 24) suggest about the act of making a covenant?
- What is the role of brutal honesty in making a covenant together?

Making a Covenant for Evangelism Together

Invite the group to turn to the "Covenant for Evangelism" (page 107) and to consider it together by following these steps:

1. Amend the *language* about evangelism found in this covenant if necessary.
2. Keep each line of this covenant to which you can agree.

3. Mark out any line of this covenant to which you cannot agree. (Brutal honesty at work!)

4. Add anything that you consider important for making this covenant together.

Closing Prayer

Invite the group to form a circle. Let the leader begin this closing prayer by praying for the person to her right. Then, going around the circle, let each person in turn pray for the person on their right. Use the prayer below as a guide, but feel free to make this prayer unique for each person involved.

Loving Creator:
Give [name] the grace to share
the joy and justice of your love.
Make [name] an evangelist of the highest order,
with open ears to listen to the stories of others,
open eyes to see your redemptive presence in our world,
and an open heart to be transformed by your love.

COVENANT
FOR EVANGELISM

We hear the call to love God and to love our neighbors as we love ourselves. We hear the call to share the joy and justice of the gospel in a world where God is already redemptively present. To answer those calls faithfully, we make a covenant to do the following with mutual support and ongoing prayer:

As a way of loving God,

we will meditate on "God's story" as it is
  hinted at through nature,
  supposed through reason,
  revealed in the scriptures,
  and incarnate in Jesus Christ.
We will look in hope for God's redemptive presence in
  the world.

As a way of loving our neighbor,

we will actively invite others to share their life stories with us,
  listening carefully to their stories as faith stories,
  celebrating their joys and mourning their sorrows,
  sharing the joy and justice of the gospel in word and deed.

As a way of loving ourselves,

we will attend to our own stories,
  celebrating the gifts that God has given us,
  facing our challenges with hope,
  trusting God's grace to provide our needs.

Notes

Session One / Diagnosing the Quandary of Evangelism

1. John Shelby Spong, *A New Christianity for a New World: Why Traditional Faith Is Dying and How a New Faith Is Being Born* (San Francisco: HarperSanFrancisco, 2001), 178.

2. "Pues Si Vivimos," Stanza 1, in *The Presbyterian Hymnal: Hymns, Psalms, and Spiritual Songs*, trans. Elise S. Eslinger (Louisville: Westminster/John Knox Press, 1990), no. 400.

3. Paul Tillich, *Systematic Theology*, vol. 2, *Existence and the Christ* (Chicago: University of Chicago Press, 1957), 47.

Session Two / The Great Commission and the Initiative of Evangelism

4. George Stroup, in the introduction to *Many Voices, One God: Being Faithful in a Pluralistic World*, ed. Walter Brueggemann and George W. Stroup (Louisville: Westminster John Knox Press, 1998), 8. Stroup's argument pertains to missions, but is applicable to evangelism as well.

Session Three / Evangelism as Conversation: Listening

5. Nick Pollard, *Evangelism Made Slightly Less Difficult: How to Interest People Who Aren't Interested* (Downers Grove, IL: InterVarsity Press, 1997), 44.

Session Four / Listening and Telling

6. Barbara Kingsolver, *The Poisonwood Bible* (New York: Harper-Flamingo, 1998).

7. Ibid., 276.

8. There are quite a number of interpretive issues just like this one that affect the way one reads the seventeenth chapter of Acts. For a brief overview of some of the translation problems with this story, as well as an articulation of the theological approach that informs my own translation, see my article on Acts 17:16–34 in *Interpretation: A Journal of Bible and Theology* 57, no. 1 (January 2003): 64–66.

9. Douglas F. Ottati, *Hopeful Realism: Reclaiming the Poetry of Theology* (Cleveland: Pilgrim Press, 1999): 69–84.

10. John Calvin, *Commentary on the Epistle of Paul the Apostle to the Corinthians*, vol. 1, trans. John Pringle (Grand Rapids: Wm. B. Eerdmans, 1948), 104.

11. William Stacy Johnson, "Re-thinking Theology: A Postmodern, Post-Holocaust, Post-Christendom Endeavor," *Interpretation: A Journal of Bible and Theology* 55, no. 1 (January 2001).

Session Five / Telling Stories Faithfully

12. Kazuo Ishiguro, *The Remains of the Day* (London: Faber and Faber, 1989).

13. The same story-within-a-larger-story motif is in Ishiguro's book *Never Let Me Go* (New York: Alfred E. Knopf, 2005). It begins as a "coming of age" story about children growing up in what might be a boarding school or an orphanage. The reader is immersed into the remembered details of the children's lives and relationships, with occasional cryptic references to the future. As it turns out, the children are clones, who are cordoned off within the school so they can be living organ donors as young adults. Suddenly, the ethical problems of cloning, human rights for cloned persons, forced organ donations, and so forth make the children's lives and relationships take on a whole new meaning.

14. Kelli Walker-Jones and Dick Hester, "A Narrative Approach to Pastor-Congregational Relationships." This article, available online at *www.divinity.duke.edu/programs/spe/articles/200508/narrative.html*, is a publication of the Sustaining Pastoral Excellence Project at Triangle Pastoral Counseling in Raleigh, North Carolina.

15. For the reference to "archeologists of hope," Walker-Jones and Hester cite the book by Gerald Monk and others, *Narrative Therapy in*

Practice: The Archaeology of Hope (San Francisco: Jossey-Bass, 1997), as an excellent resource to the whole practice of narrative therapy.

16. Kelli Walker-Jones and Dick Hester, "A Narrative Approach to Pastor-Congregational Relationships."

17. Although I am taking this phrase in a different direction, the title for this section and the use of this phrase were inspired by Walter Brueggemann's fine book *Biblical Perspectives on Evangelism: Living in a Three-Storied Universe* (Nashville: Abingdon Press, 1993).

Session Six / Witnessing to the Joy and Justice of the Gospel

18. If I am correct in this assertion, one of our future tasks will be to find new and appropriate language for describing this activity "formerly known as evangelism."

19. Hans-Georg Gadamer, *Truth and Method*, 2nd rev. ed., trans. and rev. Joel Weinsheimer and Donald G. Marshall (New York: Crossroad, 1989).

20. E. Eddie Fox and George E. Morris, *Faith-Sharing: Dynamic Christian Witnessing by Invitation*, rev. expanded ed. (Nashville: Discipleship Resources, 2002), 53.

21. Luis N. Rivera, *A Violent Evangelism: The Political and Religious Conquest of the Americas* (Louisville: Westminster/John Knox Press, 1992), 211. This text is translated from the Spanish *Evangelización y violencia: La conquista de América* (San Juan, Puerto Rico: Editorial CEMI, 1991).